FERNAND, MAGELLAN,

THE WORLD'S GREAT EXPLORERS

Ferdinand Magellan

By Jim Hargrove

◁▷ CHILDRENS PRESS ®

CHICAGO

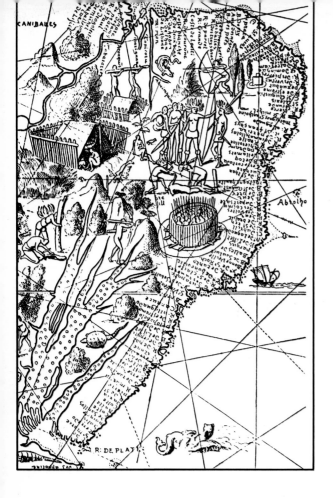

The coast of Brazil, from a map drawn around the sixteenth century. Place names are written along the coast. The interior is illustrated with the artist's idea of the Brazilian natives and their customs.

Opposite page: Historic map showing the route around the world

Project Editor: Ann Heinrichs
Designer: Lindaanne Donohoe
Typesetter: Compositors Corporation
Engraver: Liberty Photoengraving

Library of Congress Cataloging-in-Publication Data
Hargrove, Jim.
  Ferdinand Magellan / by Jim Hargrove.
    p.   cm. — (The World's great explorers)
  Bibliography : p.
  Includes index.
  Summary : The life of the Portuguese navigator and explorer who launched the first voyage around the world in the early 1500's but met his death before his men completed the expedition.
  ISBN 0-516-03051-5
  1. Magalhães, Fernão de, d. 1521—Juvenile literature. 2. Explorers—Portugal—Biography—Juvenile literature. 3. Voyages around the world—Juvenile literature. [1. Magellan, Ferdinand, d. 1521. 2. Explorers. 3. Voyages around the world.] I. Title. II. Series.
G286.M2H34 1989
910.92—dc20
[B]   89-15781
[92]   CIP
                                            AC

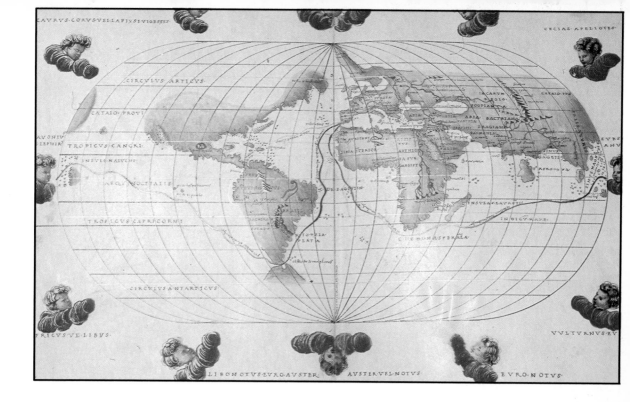

Table of Contents

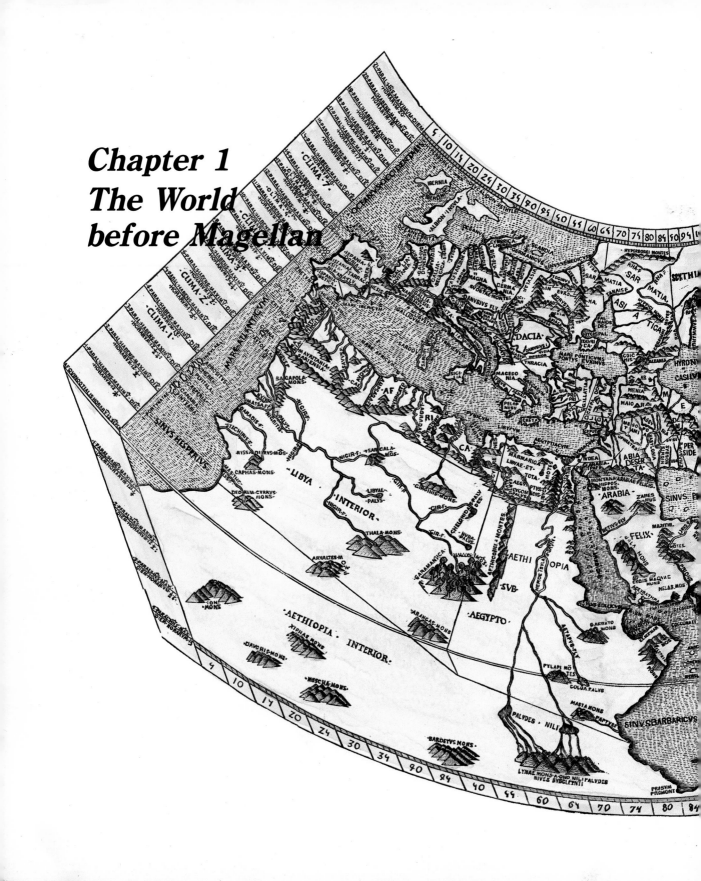

Chapter 1
The World
before Magellan

In 1480, near the time Ferdinand Magellan was born, European maps of the world had changed little in over a thousand years. The Greek scholar Claudius Ptolemaeus, better known today as Ptolemy, prepared a map of the known world in A.D. 150.

For centuries, Ptolemy's map was accepted as the best available. The early Europeans simply made copies of the map. But it was accurate only for areas around the Mediterranean Sea. North and South America, which made up the New World, had not yet been discovered. Because Ptolemy knew nothing of these lands, his map showed only Europe, Africa, and parts of Asia. A mysterious "unknown land" was drawn at the southern limit of the map. The Indian Ocean, east of Africa, was shown as a sea completely surrounded by land.

Above: Marco Polo's voyage from China in the thirteenth century. Below: A fifteenth-century concept of the world's landmasses

By the end of the fifteenth century, European mapmakers knew more about Asia than did Ptolemy. The voyages of Marco Polo and some Portuguese explorers proved that the Indian Ocean was an open sea. Western merchants began trading with China, India, and other faraway Asian lands. (These lands were known as the Orient, meaning the East.) From there, traders brought gold, silks, and spices to Europe. European rulers gave money and ships to their sailors and explorers to find faster, shorter routes to the Orient. Between four hundred and five hundred years ago, European seamen became the first people to travel around the world. They searched for gold and silver, but above all for spices such as pepper, cloves, cinnamon, and ginger.

In the northern countries of Europe, spices were rare and costly. But in Asian lands such as India and China, spices grew in abundance. A group of islands off the southeast coast of Asia became known as the Spice Islands. Today, these islands are part of Indonesia. For centuries in Europe, those fragrant spices were among the most sought-after treasures in the world.

There were good reasons why Europeans hungered after these spices. Much of the food eaten in Europe was not very tasty. Also, without refrigeration or canning, food spoiled quickly. Spices from the East made food flavorful and could disguise the taste of spoiled food. Some spices even kept meats and other foods from rotting so quickly. At the time, the best way to preserve meat was to cure it with ground salt and pepper. Salt was plentiful in Europe, but pepper was rare and valuable. In fact, only the wealthiest people could buy spices, and they were willing to pay a great deal for them.

German woodcuts made in 1537, showing a cinnamon harvest (left) and a pepper harvest (right) in the Moluccas, which were known as the Spice Islands

A Southeast Asian spice market in the 1500s

Throughout much of Europe, peppercorns were worth their weight, or more, in silver. Yet in Southeast Asia, peppercorns were so common they cost little more than other fruits and vegetables.

What made peppercorns and other spices so expensive in Europe? Merchants had to pay traders to bring the spices from the Far East to European kitchens. The long, often dangerous journey took place over land and sea. For much of this long route, the spice trade was controlled by Arab merchants.

The voyage of a single sack of pepper from the Spice Islands to western Europe covered thousands of miles. Each stage in the journey added to its price. Asian trading ships carried the pepper to the Malay Peninsula at the southern tip of the Asian mainland. Merchants had to pay a fee to the local prince before they could load the pepper into a larger ship. After a voyage across the Bay of Bengal to India, the pepper often passed from ship to ship along the coast of India until it reached the Arabian Sea. Once there, Arab and Persian ships took the spice to the Persian Gulf, near the present-day countries of Iran and Saudi Arabia. At every port, traders had to pay local taxes. On the high seas, their ships were threatened by storms and roving pirates.

Once the shipment of pepper finally reached the Persian Gulf, other traders packed it onto camels. Long caravans wound their way across the Arabian Desert. The camel drivers had to watch out for thieves and warring tribes. When at last the caravans reached the eastern shore of the Mediterranean Sea, the pepper was sold to traders from Venice. These traders brought the spices, now fabulously expensive, to the ports of Europe.

A camel caravan taking spices across the Arabian Desert

Because the spice trade meant great wealth, western European explorers tried to find a faster, cheaper sea route to the Orient. This search led to some of history's greatest sailing adventures and discoveries. In 1487 Bartolomeu Dias first rounded the southern tip of Africa. Only a few years later, in 1492, Christopher Columbus reached America. Until his death in 1506, Columbus believed he had found Asia by sailing west across the Atlantic Ocean. Vasco da Gama in 1498 reached the coast of India by traveling east around the

Christopher Columbus and his crew aboard the Santa Maria *on the morning of October 12, 1492, as land is sighted at last*

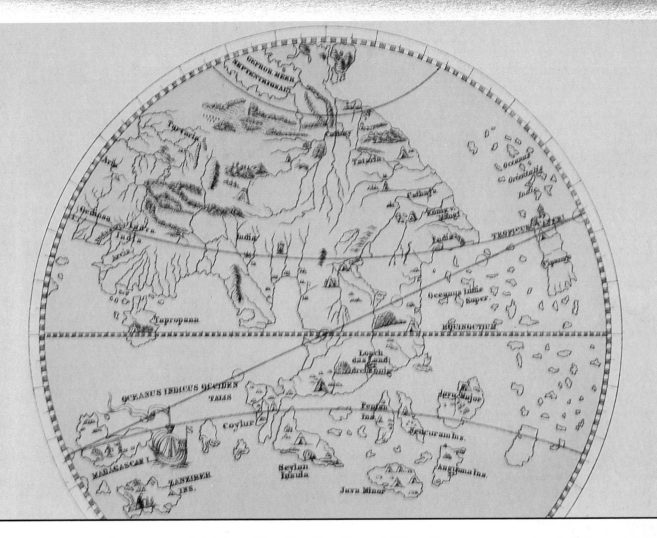

southern tip of Africa. Finally, Ferdinand Magellan, searching for a route through the New World to Asia, led the first expedition around the world. In the history of exploration, the quest for pepper is surely nothing to sneeze at!

The search for a sea route to the Orient launched what became known as the Age of Discovery. Almost within the span of Magellan's lifetime, Europeans explored the Old and New Worlds in detail.

In many ways, the small nation of Portugal, Ferdinand Magellan's homeland, was the birthplace of the Age of Discovery.

Above: A map of Eastern lands drawn in the 1400s by German geographer Martin Behaim. Below: Vasco da Gama, the first European to reach India by sea

Chapter 2
A Page in the Age
of Discovery

More than five centuries have passed since the birth of Ferdinand Magellan around 1480. Little is known about his early years. Nearly all early papers and documents about him have been lost or destroyed. Even the few details that were found may have mixed up Magellan with others who had the same last name. His name—Fernão de Magalhães in Portuguese and Fernando de Magallanes in Spanish—was very common. During his years in service to the king, half a dozen people named Magellan worked for the royal court.

No one is even sure exactly where in Portugal Magellan was born. Several cities have claimed to be the birthplace of the famous explorer. Most probably, Ferdinand was born in spring of 1480 near the city of Braga in an old watchtower called Torre de Magalhães. A French ancestor had built the tower around A.D. 1095 as a fortress against the Moors. These North African Arabs had invaded Spain and Portugal to spread their Islamic faith. By the thirteenth century, however, they had been driven out of Portugal.

Ferdinand was probably the third child of Dom Ruí Magalhães and Donha Alda de Mesquita, members of Portugal's lower nobility. Throughout his life, Ferdinand loved his older sister Isabel and older brother Diogo, with whom he shared a number of adventures.

At the time Magellan was born, the old watchtower had been partly torn down. What was left made a rather odd two-story farmhouse. The Magellan family lived upstairs, while the first floor served as a stable for farm animals. Like other European farmers, the Magellans raised cattle and grew wheat, rye, and grapes on their land.

Young Ferdinand must have had his share of chores around the family farm. He probably helped pick grapes and with his brother and sister crushed them with his bare feet to press out the juice. His father used the juice to make wine. Ferdinand may have hunted small animals with a crossbow and gathered chestnuts and acorns in the hillside forests nearby. Like everyone in the family, he must have worked long, hard hours during planting and harvest time.

Henry the Navigator

In addition to being a hardworking young man, Magellan was also very religious. He probably received training in Christian beliefs during his earliest years at home and in school. Besides going to church regularly, he may have marched in processions on religious holidays and saints' days.

Although little is known about Magellan's early life, a great deal is known about Portugal's efforts to reach India and the Orient by sea. Long before Magellan's birth, Portugal tried to take the spice trade away from the Arabs. In 1415, Portuguese troops under Prince Henry captured the Arab city of Ceuta in Morocco on the North African coast. From there, Henry learned

Caravels on the high seas

that it was possible to reach the Indian Ocean by sailing southward along the western coast of Africa. Until his death in 1460, he sent ships down the coast searching for a sea route to India.

Because of Henry's many contributions to Portuguese navigation, he became known as Prince Henry the Navigator. He helped to design the caravel, a ship whose triangular sails made it possible to sail into the wind. He first used the wind-rose compass, an early form of the modern mariner's compass. From the Arabs, Henry learned how to use the astrolabe, a device that helped sailors to determine latitude. The Portuguese prince also founded a navigation school that trained many sailors.

King John II of Portugal

After Prince Henry's death, Portuguese exploration along the west coast of Africa nearly stopped. When King John II came to the throne in 1481, he quickly decided to continue the search for a route to the Orient. He hired sea captains to explore not only the African coast but the Azores and Madeira islands in the Atlantic Ocean.

In 1482, Captain Diogo Cão sailed farther down the African coast than had any other European. He discovered the mouth of the Congo River. Shortly afterward, the Portuguese found that pepper grew in West Africa just north of the equator. Now the valuable spice could be shipped from Africa to Europe. Suddenly King John became more interested in African trade than in finding a shorter route to the East.

Only an accident made him think about the Oriental trade again. Early in 1488, a terrible storm had blown Captain Bartolomeu Dias's two caravels off course around the southern tip of Africa. The explorers were lost at sea for days. When they finally sighted the African mainland, they saw it ran to the northeast. This proved they had crossed from the western to the eastern side of Africa. The Orient lay within reach! Captain Dias was eager to continue sailing for India, but the other captains in his fleet demanded that they return to Portugal.

King John was excited by the news Dias brought home to Lisbon, Portugal's capital city. At the same time, Christopher Columbus had been trying to convince the king that Asia could be reached by sailing westward. He wanted the king to provide ships and money for the voyage. Dias's discovery made King John lose interest in Columbus's plan. The unhappy Columbus had to look for help elsewhere. Eventually, he persuaded the royal court in Spain to give him three ships.

The historic voyage of Bartolomeu Dias toward the Cape of Good Hope, Africa's southern tip

Meantime, the young boy who would become perhaps the greatest captain of them all was beginning his education. While Bartolomeu Dias rounded the southern tip of Africa, Ferdinand Magellan and his brother Diogo started school at a monastery near their home. Ferdinand was probably about eight years old at the time. Like Diogo, Ferdinand learned about Christianity as well as arithmetic and Latin. But their father knew they could receive an even better education. Because the family were members of Portugal's minor nobility, Diogo, as oldest son, was the legal heir of an aristocratic family. He would inherit his father's title and the family lands. As a legal heir, he was also entitled to a free education in the Portuguese royal court.

The Braganzas, relatives of King John II, ruled Portugal for several hundred years. Joao II (above), the 8th Duke of Braganza, became King John IV in the year 1640.

King John must have liked Ruí Magalhães and his family. He allowed not only Diogo but, soon after, Ferdinand to be educated at the royal court. In 1492, the year Columbus first sailed to the New World, Ferdinand followed his brother to Queen Leonor's court in Lisbon. There he entered the school for pages, as young boys serving the royal court were called. In return for their education, pages ran errands and did other work for members of the king's court.

In the late 1400s, Portugal had two royal courts. In one court was King John, who was constantly in danger of being killed by rival relatives called the Braganzas. To protect himself, the king hired armed guards and moved often from place to place.

Queen Leonor ruled over Portugal's other royal court. Although originally located in Lisbon, her court also moved often. This was to avoid not only the Braganzas but an even deadlier threat—the plague. A great epidemic of the plague had broken out in Portugal. The queen fled to a new castle or monastery whenever the dreaded disease broke out near her court.

Despite these problems, Queen Leonor's court offered a fine education. As in other European courts, the young men learned the skills of hunting, jousting, and swordsmanship along with music, dance, and academic subjects. But the students also learned astronomy, mapmaking, navigation, and naval science. These subjects had been part of the navigation school founded by Prince Henry the Navigator.

King John wanted the young students to become skilled mariners for Portugal. He hired seasoned sailors as teachers. These men had firsthand experience at sea. The skills Ferdinand learned at the royal school helped him become a master sailor and navigator.

Young men attending schools in European royal courts learned grammar, arithmetic, geometry, astronomy, and other subjects.

But Ferdinand also had problems at the school. Duke Manuel, brother to Queen Leonor, was in charge of all the pages. He was a skilled athlete and a favorite of the queen. Yet Manuel was also related to the Braganza family, rivals to the Portuguese throne. He probably secretly hoped the Braganzas' plots against King John would succeed. He may have felt that people loyal to the king—such as the Magellan family—were his enemies.

From the moment Ferdinand Magellan entered the school for pages, Duke Manuel took a dislike to him. Crown Prince Afonso, the only son of King John and Queen Leonor and heir to the Portuguese throne, had been killed shortly before Ferdinand entered the school. The prince may have been assassinated by agents of the Braganzas. Duke Manuel was now in a position to become king of Portugal if King John should die. The duke's dislike of Ferdinand and his family lasted many years and eventually had tragic results for Ferdinand.

The return of Columbus from his voyage to the New World

Young Magellan had been in school for only a year when the royal court received astounding news. In March 1493, bad weather forced Christopher Columbus into the port of Lisbon. He told an amazed royal court that he had reached the Orient by sailing west across the Atlantic Ocean. Columbus had brought a few American Indians with him, and they seemed to look like Asians. Meeting with the Italian sailor, King John may have tried to hide his embarrassment. After all, Columbus had first asked to sail for Portugal. Only after John rejected his plan did Columbus go to Spain.

According to an old treaty between Spain and Portugal, the lands that Columbus discovered in the western Atlantic belonged to Spain. In 1493, Pope Alexander VI, head of the Catholic Church and a Spaniard, made the Spanish claim more official. The pope drew an imaginary line from north to south about 575 miles (925 kilometers) west of the Azores islands. Spain would own all land discovered west of this line. Ships from other countries were not allowed to cross the line without Spain's permission. Columbus's discovery—including all of the Americas—lay in Spanish territory.

King John realized he had made a great mistake by not listening to Columbus. He had to make sure that more of the new lands to be discovered would fall on Portugal's side of the line. Perhaps he could change the treaty. Using his diplomatic skills, and a few bribes to Spanish diplomats, King John managed to get a new treaty with Spain that was more favorable to Portugal.

On June 7, 1494, the Treaty of Tordesillas changed the pope's first ruling. This treaty moved the dividing line about 800 miles (1,287 kilometers) to the west. Although not all the lands included were known at the time, the treaty gave India, Indonesia, Africa, and Brazil to Portugal. Spain received most of the Americas and the Pacific Ocean, not yet seen by any Europeans except a few traders and travelers like Marco Polo.

Columbus's voyage, and reports of the Treaty of Tordesillas, must have been exciting news for the pages at the Portuguese court. Even more stirring were King John's plans for Portugal's own voyages of discovery. Soon after the Treaty of Tordesillas was signed, the king made preparations for two separate sea voyages to India. The expeditions would start out in opposite directions!

The young pages at Queen Leonor's court must have listened to reports of these voyages with awe. They had studied long hours to learn how to navigate on open sea. Many surely dreamed of exciting naval careers. But these hopes were soon dealt a crushing blow.

King Manuel of Portugal

King John, the target of assassins for years, was finally poisoned and died at the age of forty. The Braganzas became the royal family of Portugal. In October 1495, Duke Manuel, no friend of Ferdinand Magellan, was crowned the Portuguese king. Noble families loyal to King John found their homes and lands taken away from them. Many fled to Spain. Jews also were banished by the new king. They had the choice of being baptized in the Christian faith, fleeing the country, or being executed.

For a time, King Manuel lost interest in the voyages of discovery that King John had planned. Italian traders and shipbuilders quickly stepped in and began preparing for these voyages themselves. The new Portuguese king also sent fewer ships to trade for African pepper. But other merchants, led by the Spanish pepper trader Cristóbal de Haro, were eager to take trade away from Portugal. At last, alarmed by these foreign merchants, King Manuel decided to renew his country's efforts to find a sea route to India.

Soon after he came to the throne, the new king moved the school for pages to his own royal court. Ferdinand Magellan was probably at the ceremony held on July 8, 1497, to launch Portugal's first voyage of discovery. The king put twenty-eight-year-old Vasco da Gama in charge of the expedition.

Ferdinand Magellan, then about seventeen years old, had finished his school days as a page. He got a job as a clerk in the naval department of King Manuel's palace. He probably helped gather provisions and other materials for da Gama's great trip to India. The voyage became one of the most important events in world history.

Da Gama's small fleet was gone for two years and two months. In September 1499, only two of da Gama's four ships returned to Portugal. But da Gama brought

Portuguese explorer Vasco da Gama meets with the zamorin of Calicut in India.

exciting news. He had reached India—weathering storms, mutinies, and attacks by Arabs and Indians. He had lost two of his ships and two-thirds of his crew, including his own brother. Despite these hardships, da Gama managed to bring back a small cargo of valuable spices, more than enough to pay for the voyage.

For thousands of years, the people of Spain and Portugal had known little of the world beyond the lands around the Mediterranean Sea. By the early 1500s, Spanish and Portuguese sailors had discovered sea routes to Asia and the Americas. Christopher Columbus made four voyages across the Atlantic Ocean, each time believing he had reached Asia. By 1507, however, the princes, navigators, and scholars of Europe knew he had actually discovered an entirely New World.

Amerigo Vespucci (above) explored the coast of Brazil and returned to Europe claiming to have discovered a new continent. Although Columbus reached the New World earlier, he thought he had found Asia. Because of Vespucci's vivid descriptions of the new continent, the Americas were named after him.

After da Gama's voyage, King Manuel sent many expeditions to India along the new eastern sea route. The king also decided to find a westward route to the Orient. On March 15, 1501, a fleet of four ships under João da Nova set sail for Brazil in the New World. Less than two months later, King Manuel sent a second and a third fleet to Brazil. The third fleet, commanded by the Italian captain Amerigo Vespucci, was told to find a passage through the New World to Asia. Vespucci failed. But he sparked the search for a passage that would not be discovered until Ferdinand Magellan reached the New World.

Portugal's new wealth brought great changes to the country in only a few years. The spices, dyes, and other Oriental riches sold to other European countries made many Portuguese merchants and nobles rich. They built fine new homes, many as grand as palaces. Fancy carriages crowded the streets, carrying passengers who wore the costliest furs and silks.

Not surprisingly, most of Portugal's young men were eager to travel to the Orient to earn their fortunes. The trickle of adventurers soon turned into a flood. From 1500 to 1525, nearly eighty thousand Portuguese men sailed abroad—almost one-third of the entire male population! Many never returned. Many others who stayed died of the plague. As a result, Portugal did not have enough skilled workers to fill all the jobs at home.

Although Magellan longed to join the adventurers going to sea, he could not get permission from King Manuel. He was not allowed to join da Gama's second trip to India in 1502 or any other voyage. The king's dislike for the young clerk seemed certain to ruin Magellan's dreams.

For a few years, the young man worked in India House. This was a royal agency that collected taxes on all goods brought into or sent out of the country. Finally, in 1505, Ferdinand got the chance he had been waiting for. King Manuel decided to send a large, armed fleet to East Africa and India. The expedition was to protect Portuguese trading ships from Arab attacks. They would also build several forts along the coasts of Africa and India.

The skilled captain Francisco de Almeida was in charge of the expedition. The captain asked the king to include people on the voyage who had worked in India House. Ferdinand Magellan, his brother Diogo, and his cousin Francisco Serrão all were given permission to sail with the expedition. At last Magellan could join his countrymen in the fabled lands of the East.

Many thousands of Europeans died of the plague in the fourteenth, fifteenth, and sixteenth centuries. This woodcut shows a physician treating a plague victim. He breathes through a vinegar-soaked sponge for protection.

Chapter 3
The Reluctant
Empire Builder

The largest fleet ever to leave Portugal made ready to sail from Lisbon harbor on March 25, 1505. In all, the twenty-two ships under Francisco de Almeida's command carried 1,980 men, most of them soldiers. A few, including Ferdinand Magellan, were called gentleman adventurers. They served without pay.

At dawn a Mass was held to pray for a safe voyage. The sailors' relatives and loved ones who gathered at the harbor did not know if they would see their husbands, brothers, sons, or friends again. All hands had signed on for three years of service. In a number of earlier voyages to India, fewer than half the men ever returned. The festive music of trumpets and the roar of the ships' guns could not hide the heartache that those left behind must have felt. As they watched, the fleet set sail with the falling tide.

The list of passengers for the great fleet does not tell which ship carried Ferdinand Magellan. He was probably on board one of the smaller vessels. Captain-General Francisco de Almeida commanded the large caravel in the lead. The captain skillfully held his fleet together during the long voyage down the African coast.

The fleet reached the southern tip of Africa on June 21, 1505, almost three months after it left Lisbon. In the Northern Hemisphere this date marks the summer solstice, the longest day of the year and the start of summer. But the fleet was now far south of the equator, in the Southern Hemisphere. Here, the same date marks the shortest day of the year and the onset of winter.

With their frail ships bobbing in the high waves of the windblown sea, the sailors suffered through terrible cold. Ice formed on the ships' rigging and huge waves swept nine men overboard to watery graves. For two weeks, no cooking fires could be lit aboard the ships.

At last the fleet sailed into the Indian Ocean and far up the east coast of Africa, leaving the cold days and nights behind. The ships were dragged onto the beach and turned on their sides so the hulls could be cleaned. Almeida ordered the men to gather food and fresh water to store on board. The time was near for the captain-general to carry out the king's orders.

King Manuel wanted to control all trade between Europe and the East. To do so, he planned to conquer most of the African and Indian coasts and to build Portuguese colonies and fortresses there. This would drive out the Arab and Indian traders who lived on the coasts. King Manuel would no longer have to pay these traders for passing on the spices. By controlling the coastal cities, he could gain even larger profits.

The Portuguese plan was simple. Along the trade route, Almeida's fleet would seize all important straits, or narrow water passageways. At the same time, they would build forts on the east coast of Africa and the west coast of India. Almeida's ships carried great stores of timber for building the fortresses. From these sea and land bases, the Portuguese would be able to dominate all

Arab slave traders plundered East Africa for men and women they could kidnap and sell as slaves.

trade in the Indian Ocean. They could also conquer nearby cities and set up Portuguese colonies. In a few cases, the colonies lasted well into the twentieth century.

Almeida's fleet began to carry out King Manuel's strategy with astonishing fury. Sailing up the east coast of Africa, they attacked an Arab slave-trading stronghold at Kilwa in what is now Tanzania. They slaughtered most of the Arab men and burned Kilwa and nearby coastal towns to the ground. As soon as the cities were destroyed, Almeida and part of the fleet continued north. There they destroyed more Arab cities along the African coast. A number of Portuguese ships, including Magellan's, were left behind. They patrolled the coast, making sure they controlled all trade in the area.

By December 1505, Magellan's skills as a mariner had been noticed by Nuno Vaz Pereira, commander of the Portuguese patrol. He promoted Magellan to the position of pilot's assistant on one of the patrol ships. When Pereira was transferred to the west coast of India in 1507, the new pilot's assistant went with him.

Ferdinand Magellan arrived in India in October 1507. Only nine years had passed since Vasco da Gama's historic voyage first opened up the sea route between Europe and India. Already, the Portuguese, led by Almeida, were trying to settle parts of the Indian coast. At the city of Cochin near the southern tip of India's west coast, the Portuguese had built a church, a hospital, and several government buildings.

The rajah, or ruler, of Cochin was friendly to the Portuguese. But a number of other Indian princes were not, including the zamorin of Calicut, the king of

Calcutta in the sixteenth century

Village on an island in the Indian Ocean

Cambay, and the rajah of Goa. Besides these hostile Indians, the Portuguese invaders faced another powerful enemy in the Indian Ocean. For countless years, Arab traders had made fortunes by trading with Indian merchants and bringing their goods to the Middle East and Europe. The Arabs were eager to rid the Indian Ocean of these newcomers from Europe.

For a time in 1507 and 1508, Magellan sailed with an expedition to Ceylon (now Sri Lanka), an island near the southeastern tip of India. The expedition was soon called back to rejoin Almeida's main fleet in the Indian Ocean. Almeida had been given the title of viceroy of India. That meant he acted as the highest official for King Manuel in India. The returning sailors soon learned that Almeida's son had been killed early in 1508 in a battle at the Indian city of Dabul.

33

Viceroy Almeida's anger over his son's death seemed boundless. Under his command, Portuguese soldiers burned Dabul and killed every man, woman, and child living in the city. Almeida then turned his rage toward the enemy's ships at sea. He searched for the Indian and Arab fleet that he knew was somewhere in the Indian Ocean.

He found the ships on February 2, 1509, near the small island of Diu off the northwest coast of India. Anchored there was a huge fleet of more than twenty thousand men and two hundred Indian and Arab ships. Although Almeida's fleet was only one-tenth the size of the enemy's, the Portuguese commander attacked at once. In the fierce battle, both sides lost many men and ships. At last, the Arab and Indian ships turned and fled. The Portuguese had won!

But they paid a high price for victory. Captain Nuno Vaz Pereira, Magellan's powerful ally, was killed. Magellan himself was badly wounded, and for days his friends expected him to die. It was six weeks before he could be moved from Diu to the hospital at Cochin. Throughout the spring and early summer of 1509, Magellan slowly recovered.

After regaining his health, Magellan stayed in India for a few more weeks. He served as a mounted knight, probably helping to protect the tiny Portuguese colony along the coast. Attacks came from neighboring Indians, some riding armor-covered elephants. Magellan may have had some trouble returning to service at sea. His chief ally, Captain Pereira, was dead, and even Viceroy Almeida had fallen into disgrace. Almeida was replaced by a new viceroy of India, Afonso de Albuquerque. Soon, however, Magellan got another chance for adventure at sea.

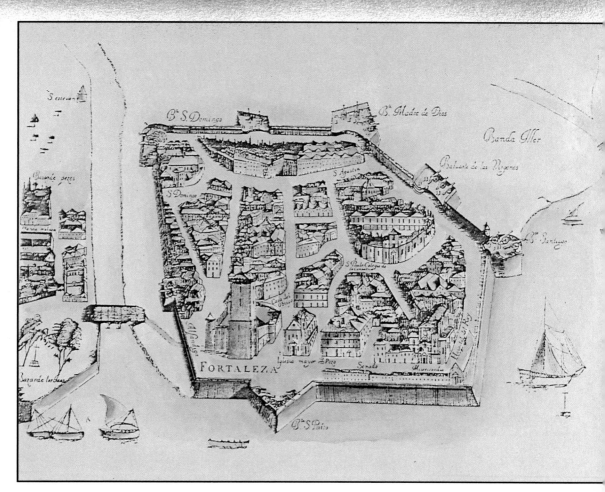

The fortified city of Malacca on the Malay Peninsula

Captain Diogo Lopes de Sequeira, a personal friend of King Manuel, arrived in Cochin. He carried secret orders to lead a fleet two thousand miles east to the city of Malacca on the Malay Peninsula of Southeast Asia. Magellan and his cousin Francisco Serrão eagerly joined the expedition.

Sequeira's fleet of five ships crossed the mouth of the Bay of Bengal. On September 11, 1509, twenty-three days after leaving India, they announced their arrival at Malacca with a blast of ships' trumpets. For Europeans, the Malay Peninsula was a fabled land, deep in the Orient and not far from the Spice Islands. No other Portuguese had ever sailed so far to the east. There they found a crowded harbor and a beautiful, bustling city.

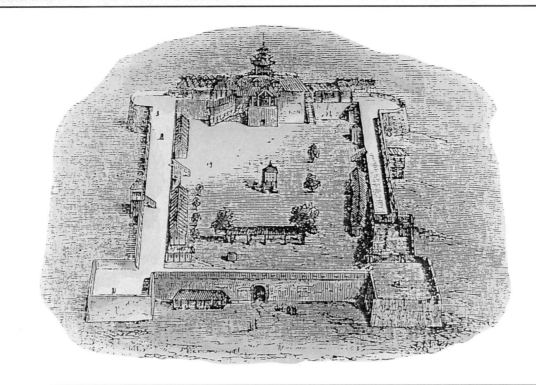

A fortified castle on Amboina, one of the many islands in the Molucca group

"Truly there are more ships in this harbor than any place on earth," wrote one of the Portuguese captains. In the harbor, Magellan and his fellow sailors could see boats from all over the East: junks from China, dhows from the Middle East, and scores of local sampans.

The view of the city of Malacca was even more exciting. Lining the harbor were high walls topped with countless brass cannons pointing out to sea. Behind these walls gleamed the domed tops of temples and mosques rising above the mansions and gardens of rich traders. At the crest of a steep hill stood the magnificent palace of Sultan Mohammed, the ruler of Malacca.

For sailors, this spot on the Malay Peninsula was the most important strait of the East. Ships sailing between the South China Sea and the Indian Ocean usually had to pass through the Strait of Malacca. Likewise, ships traveling to and from China, Japan, the Spice Islands, and Southeast Asia also had to use the strait.

Sailors and traders from Malacca spoke in dozens of different languages and traded in a wide range of goods. They brought huge cargoes of spices from the Spice Islands, rubies from Ceylon, ivory from Siam (Thailand), porcelain and brassware from China, fancy swords and fine cloth and pepper from India, and slaves with wooden sticks through their noses from Borneo.

For a time the ruler of Malacca, Sultan Mohammed, pretended to be friends with the Portuguese. Captain Sequeira and Sultan Mohammed gave gifts to each as a sign of friendship. But Magellan and some of the other officers aboard the fleet felt something was wrong. They visited the mainland, trying to discover any secret plots against the Portuguese. At first, they found none.

But the crafty sultan had little use for the Portuguese. He was planning to seize the men along with their ships and the goods they carried. The sultan tricked the Portuguese into bringing all their goods ashore. In secret, he gathered his soldiers and war elephants near the harbor and hid a fleet of sampans in a nearby cove.

Many Eastern rulers used elephants in warfare. These Indian elephants are outfitted for a battle.

Afonso de Albuquerque, viceroy of India

The sultan attacked early the next morning. The Portuguese fleet had to fight its way out of the harbor through dozens of small sampans. Sixty Portuguese sailors were killed on shore. Ferdinand Magellan was one of the last to make it back to the caravels. The crippled fleet headed for India. The Portuguese vowed they would be back to fight again.

But the new viceroy of India, Afonso de Albuquerque, was eager to fight the Arabs in India. Arabs known as Muslims had spread their religion, Islam, throughout much of Asia. The Christian countries of Europe believed that Islam had to be stopped. In many eastern lands, more people were converting to Islam than to Christianity. Afonso felt it was his duty to drive the Muslim Arabs out or to kill them in battle. He led one of the greatest massacres in the history of warfare.

Early in 1510, Portuguese troops under Albuquerque had conquered and then lost the Arab seaport of Goa on the west coast of India. In November of that year, Albuquerque attacked again, this time showing no mercy. Over three days, his soldiers slaughtered more than eight thousand Arabs, including old people and newborn babies.

Ferdinand Magellan was among the Portuguese who attacked Goa that November. But he probably did not take part in the bloodshed. In those days, soldiers were rewarded after a battle, but Magellan received nothing. If he had joined in the killing, he would have been paid.

Yet Magellan did receive something that meant far more to him than money. He was made captain of his own ship. When Albuquerque's fleet set sail from Goa to Malacca on March 31, 1511, Magellan commanded one of the caravels.

The Portuguese now sought revenge for the attack by

Sultan Mohammed a year and a half earlier. In August 1511, they captured Malacca and wounded the sultan, who fled from his palace on the back of an elephant.

Albuquerque allowed each of his captains to select a personal slave from the conquered people of Malacca. Ferdinand Magellan chose a black slave boy and named him Henrique de Malacca, Henry of Malacca. The two stayed together until Magellan's death.

Magellan remained in Malacca for about a year and a half. During this time, he had one more adventure. Some of the Portuguese wanted to know what lay east of the Spice Islands. Magellan sailed with them, serving as a navigator on a caravel. When he returned to Malacca, he said little about what they had discovered. His ship probably sailed northeast of the Malay Peninsula through the South China Sea. Today it is believed that he reached the Philippine Islands. Magellan would not see these islands again until his great voyage around the world.

During his time in the East, Magellan's skill in navigation and astronomy, plus his uncommon honesty, led to trouble. In a written report about his voyage, Magellan pointed out an alarming fact. His measurements seemed to show that the eastern islands he had visited, *even the Spice Islands themselves*, did not belong to Portugal! These lands lay inside the part of the world reserved for Spain by the Treaty of Tordesillas. King Manuel and other Portuguese officials were very angry when they heard the news. They agreed it was unthinkable that Spain should own any Eastern lands—especially the Spice Islands.

The man who reported the unthinkable was stripped of his command as captain. King Manuel ordered Magellan to return to Portugal in disgrace.

Chapter 4
The Subject of Kings

After serving in the Orient for eight years, Ferdinand Magellan, now thirty-three years old, returned by ship to Lisbon in 1513. He must have been amazed at how the city had changed during his absence.

Once a cluster of tiny fishing villages, Lisbon was now the busiest port in all Europe. The city boasted magnificent mansions, government buildings, and churches, all paid for by the Asian trade. In a great public square stood King Manuel's elegant new palace, whose wide stairway led down to the water. Hundreds of sailing ships of every design and from nearly every country lined the harbor where the Tagus River met the Atlantic Ocean.

For its newfound wealth, Portugal owed a debt of thanks to men such as Ferdinand Magellan. But when the adventurer visited the royal palace, he learned his years of service meant nothing to the court. Magellan entered the palace and wandered through long, empty halls. Finally he found a minor official who carried a list of people serving the king. The well-dressed official did not even recognize Magellan's name. When he finally found the name on his list, he made fun of Magellan's rank as a junior squire. Magellan had held this position when he had left Portugal in 1505. The sea captain angrily replied that he expected a quick promotion.

"You will be lucky to be advanced at all," the official said, "for you have been absent from your post for many years." The meaning was clear. Men who traveled abroad and risked their lives to bring Portugal the riches of the Orient did not earn special favors. Instead, they ranked lower than government servants in elegant clothes who performed minor duties in the palace.

Magellan also found many changes at India House, where he had once worked. In place of captains, sailors, and spice traders, the building was now staffed with lawyers, government officials, and bankers. Some of these people even plotted to steal the valuables that Magellan brought back from Asia.

To make matters worse, Magellan's salary was cut in half. The king refused to let him join the next sea voyage east. Desperate, Magellan offered to serve in North Africa, where the Portuguese were battling their longtime Arab enemies. He was granted this request. As part of this venture, he became the assistant of a famed Portuguese navigator, John of Lisbon.

Several nations formed companies to deal in goods from Africa, India, and the Far East. Merchants in The Netherlands, for instance, formed the East India Company, whose trading house in Amsterdam is shown here.

Bustling maritime activity at the seaport of Lisbon

John and Magellan became close friends. During a battle in North Africa, Magellan was wounded when a spear tore into his right knee. The deep wound healed, but he walked with a limp for the rest of his life.

By the summer of 1516, when he returned to Portugal, Magellan was almost out of money. Although a minor nobleman, his salary remained small. His fortune in Oriental goods had been stolen, and he was now lame. Like a common beggar, he decided to see King Manuel on his knees to ask for help.

Manuel still held a grudge against Magellan from the time he had been a page in the queen's court. The king certainly had not forgotten about Magellan's report suggesting that Portugal's newfound lands might belong to Spain. Their meeting was one of the most unhappy events in Magellan's life.

On certain days of the week, the king listened to pleas from his common subjects. Magellan bribed a royal usher to put his name on the list of people seeking favors. Late in the day, his name was finally called. Magellan knelt meekly before King Manuel and asked for a tiny raise in pay. He pointed out that he had served Portugal faithfully for twenty years. But Manuel flatly refused to give him any more money.

Magellan may have known his first request would be turned down. But he had other favors to ask. Could the king give him command of a royal caravel? This was a good position for a sea veteran like himself. Manuel again said no. He added that he had no use for Magellan's services at all. The king even turned down Magellan's plea to sail on a privately owned ship.

Magellan could hardly believe his ears. Angry and confused, the unlucky captain blurted out a final plea.

"May I then have permission to serve another king?"

"Serve anyone you like, clubfoot!" Manuel replied coldly. "Your service is a matter of indifference to us."

The king delivered one last insult to his subject. Custom required Magellan to kiss the monarch's hand before leaving the royal presence. But Manuel yanked his hand out of Magellan's reach. The captain tried to hide his shame as he backed away from the king. His bad leg made him stumble.

"Quit faking that pitiful limp," shouted one of the dandies surrounding the king. The court broke out into scornful laughter as Magellan fled from the palace.

No man in all of Portugal was more miserable than Magellan that night in 1516. In a hurry to leave Lisbon, he boarded a ship that same evening and sailed north to Pôrto near old Torre de Magalhães. He spent months in the waterfront taverns of Pôrto. Perhaps he tried to

drown his disgrace and sorrow in tankards of warm ale.

Pôrto was filled with out-of-work sailors. Some, like Magellan, had served in the Orient only to be spurned by King Manuel. Surely some of them wondered about the chances of finding work in neighboring Spain. Those who talked about leaving kept an eye out for King Manuel's spies. The king did not like his sailors to work for other countries.

In March 1517, Magellan's friend John of Lisbon sailed to Pôrto and found his unhappy comrade. John knew that his old friend deserved better treatment from the king. The news he brought turned out to be the first step in a great change of fortune for Magellan.

John began by bringing his friend up-to-date on the westward voyages of discovery. Starting in 1514, John had sailed westward across the Atlantic to Brazil. He had followed the coastline southward for many miles. At a certain spot, he believed he had found a passage, *el paso*, through the Americas to Asia.

The earliest known engraving of natives of the New World, showing inhabitants of the northern coast of South America as described by Portuguese explorers

As more new lands were discovered, mapmakers were able to fill in more details of the known world. This map, while highly detailed, omits that part of the west coast of South America that had not yet been explored.

Like most educated Europeans of the time, both men knew the world was round. But they thought it was much smaller than it really was. The Pacific Ocean, the world's largest body of water, was unknown to them. Both men believed that the Spice Islands and Asia were only a short distance west of the Americas.

John of Lisbon took a great risk to help his friend. Without the knowledge of King Manuel, he sneaked Magellan into the king's mapmaking room in the spring of 1517. There Magellan saw and copied a famous globe created by a German mapmaker. This globe showed a passage—*el paso*—at the exact spot in South America where John of Lisbon had described it. It was further proof to Magellan that a passage must exist through the Americas.

A few months later, another old friend visited Magellan. Duarte Barbosa, also serving the Portuguese crown, had sailed with Magellan in the Orient. Upon returning to Portugal in 1517, Barbosa, too, had been badly treated by King Manuel. In Pôrto, the two outcasts talked about an exciting new plan.

Duarte's wealthy uncle, Diogo Barbosa, knew the seventeen-year-old king of Spain, Charles I, and other Spanish nobles. Duarte and Diogo Barbosa had also heard that there was a strait through South America. The men wanted to discover a western route to the Spice Islands. They believed Magellan would make the perfect leader of an expedition. Perhaps the king of Spain would think so, too.

View of a port city along the Portuguese coast

Magellan quickly agreed to move to Spain. He left on October 12, 1517, and never returned. It was a move that, in time, the Portuguese would deeply resent.

Magellan, on the other hand, must have welcomed the change. In Spain he had a chance for a great new maritime adventure. Also in Spain was Lady Beatriz Caldeira Barbosa. She lived at her parents' magnificent mansion known as the Alcázar. Even before Magellan had met the young lady, her father Diogo had arranged for the Portuguese captain to marry her. The fact that she was beautiful, intelligent, and extremely wealthy made Magellan eager to marry.

The rich bride and the penniless groom were married in December 1517, shortly after Magellan arrived in Spain. In two years, Beatriz bore Ferdinand's two children. One died soon after birth. The other, a son named Rodrigo, lived less than five years. Even that brief time was more than Magellan had yet to live. He was now entering the final years of his life. In the short time left to him, he would lead the greatest sea adventure the world had ever known.

Ferdinand and Beatriz spent only two years together before Magellan left on his final voyage. They were the happiest years of his life.

Diogo Barbosa introduced his new son-in-law to important members of Spanish society. Among them were many aristocrats, bankers, and powerful clergymen who wanted to find a western route to Asia. One of these people was the spice trader and banker Cristóbal de Haro, well known in both Spain and Portugal. Haro decided to form an alliance with Magellan.

The captain had already become partners with another Portuguese outcast from King Manuel's court— Ruí de Faleiro. Faleiro's skills in astronomy and mapmaking could be of great use to the explorers. Magellan and Faleiro would share equally in any discoveries made on the voyage.

The Barbosas, Faleiro, Haro, and others persuaded high-ranking Spanish officials to let Magellan talk with King Charles. A nobleman of the Spanish court prepared Magellan for the meeting. The captain learned about the likes and dislikes of the young king. King Charles was told many things about Magellan, too: The Portuguese captain had noble ancestors, was a Christian crusader who had fought the Muslims, had been wounded three times in the service of Portugal, and yet remained poor after all his sacrifices.

Seventeen-year-old King Charles I of Spain

The careful planning produced a splendid meeting. At the beginning, Magellan stressed that he had received permission from King Manuel to serve another country. This was important, because the king of Spain did not want trouble with the king of neighboring Portugal. Magellan then explained his long-held belief that the Spice Islands, according to the Treaty of Tordesillas, really belonged to Spain.

For a time, Magellan and King Charles spoke through interpreters. Although Charles was king of Spain, he had been born in the city of Ghent, now a part of Belgium. Spanish was not his native tongue. Soon, however, the king dismissed the interpreters and began speaking directly to Magellan in his halting Spanish. This was a sign that he liked Magellan.

Ruí de Faleiro was also at the meeting. He used his astronomical charts to show that the Spice Islands lay within Spanish territory. Magellan then gave the king a

The city of Ghent, Belgium, birthplace of King Charles

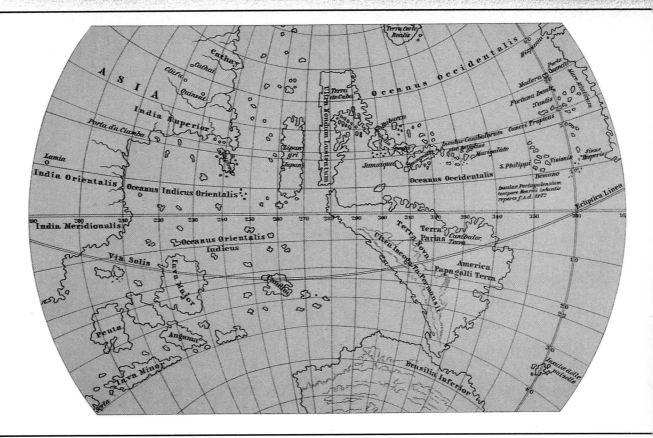

beautifully painted leather globe. It may have been a copy of the globe that Magellan examined in the Portuguese court.

The sphere showed Europe, Asia, Africa, and what was known of the New World. The great expanse of the Pacific Ocean, undiscovered at the time, was not on the map. Also, one part of the known area of South America was left blank. Magellan explained that this was where he believed *el paso*, the passage through the Americas, was located. It had been left blank to prevent other explorers from finding it first.

As a final touch, Magellan introduced his slave, Henry of Malacca. He also brought in Henry's wife, a slave girl from the Indonesian island of Sumatra. Henry addressed the king with a short speech in the Malayan language.

A map drawn by German mapmaker Johannes Schöner

King Charles must have been greatly impressed by Magellan. On March 22, 1518, he signed an agreement to supply money for the expedition. Magellan and Faleiro were made commanders, with the power of life and death over all members of the crew. The king promoted them to the rank of captain-general. They were given good salaries and a share in any profits from the trip.

Ferdinand Magellan threw all his energy into preparing for the great voyage to come. He set up headquarters in the Spanish city of Seville along the banks of the Guadalquivir River. With the king's money, he bought five second-hand ships for the trip. The largest was the *San Antonio*, followed by the *Trinidad*, the smaller *Victoria* and *Concepción*, and the smallest ship, the *Santiago*.

Seville, Spain

The Victoria, *the only ship in Magellan's fleet that survived*

Under Magellan's watchful eye, all five ships were made ready for the longest journey ever taken. Magellan inspected every sail, rope, timber, and weapon placed aboard the ships. He purchased enough food to feed the crew for two years. Rations included nearly a quarter-million pounds (113,400 kilograms) of biscuits, seventy-two thousand pounds (32,659 kilograms) of salted beef, fifty-seven thousand pounds (25,855 kilograms) of salted pork, and so on. Unfortunately, no one at the time realized the need for citrus fruits. Rich in vitamin C, these foods could prevent scurvy, a cause of death for many sailors.

But for now Magellan had other problems to worry about. King Manuel had heard about Magellan's voyage and did everything he could to ruin it. He sent spies to Seville to steal the captain's supplies. Others spread lies about the captain-general among the Spanish sailors and dock workers.

Magellan also had trouble with his Spanish friends and supporters. He wanted to make a voyage of discovery. The others were more interested in trading with merchants on the Spice Islands. They put their own supplies on board Magellan's ships. Cristóbal de Haro made sure they carried goods such as copper bracelets, colored bells, combs, fishhooks, and imitation jewels that could be traded for spices.

The Spaniards also wanted their own captains and officers to command the ships. These men had no desire to discover new lands. In fact, many did not even know how to navigate at sea! Magellan could not stop key positions in his fleet from going to these court dandies. Fortunately, King Charles allowed him to hire a number of skilled Portuguese seamen. They made up the capable core of his crew.

The fleet was originally set to sail from Seville in the autumn of 1518. But delay after delay prevented them from leaving. Magellan even lost his partner, Ruí de Faleiro. King Charles promised Faleiro he could lead a second expedition. The voyage never took place, and Faleiro missed out on Magellan's historic journey.

Another man joined the expedition at the last moment. He was a young Italian nobleman, Antonio Francesco Pigafetta. Throughout the long voyage, the Italian kept a diary of the entire adventure. This wonderful diary has survived through the centuries. Without Pigafetta's written accounts, far less of the great

Sixteenth-century Flemish woodcut of a fleet of ships taking off on a voyage

voyage would be known today. Magellan seems to have enjoyed the young Italian's company. He allowed him to travel on his own ship, the *Trinidad*.

After more than a year of delays, King Charles finally lost patience and ordered the expedition to sail. On August 10, 1519, the fleet of five ships left the harbor, sailed to the mouth of Guadalquivir River, and stopped before reaching the Atlantic. Magellan had discovered that many supplies had been stolen. It took nearly a month to get new provisions. Only then was the voyage ready to begin.

Chapter 5
A Troubled Voyage
across the Atlantic

On September 20, cannons boomed a farewell to those left behind on shore. The fleet of five ships under Captain-General Ferdinand Magellan finally sailed into the Atlantic Ocean. A total of 241 men manned the fleet.

Magellan invented a way to make sure the ships would stay together at night or in storms. On the rear deck of the *Trinidad*, a large wooden torch burned brightly. The captains could see the light in daytime or darkness. Other torches were used to signal changes in direction or to show which sails to alter. As the fleet sailed down the coast of Africa, Magellan carefully signaled the other ships.

Six days after setting sail, the fleet anchored off the little island of Tenerife, one of the Canary Islands near the West African coast. It was here that Magellan received a grim warning by messenger from his father-in-law, Diogo Barbosa.

A small, swift-sailing boat brought Magellan an urgent letter. In it, Barbosa warned that three of the Spanish captains were plotting to kill Magellan once the voyage was under way. Friends of the three captains had been overheard boasting about the plot. The assassins were Juan de Cartagena, captain of the *San Antonio*; Gaspar de Quesada, the *Concepción*'s captain; and Luis de Mendoza, captain of the *Victoria*. Barbosa also wrote that the three captains, under Cartagena's leadership, planned to take command of the fleet.

Magellan wrote back, thanking his father-in-law for the warning. He noted that he would continue to serve King Charles and added, "to this end I will offer my life." Alerted to the plot, the captain-general now had to defend both his life and his command.

Cartagena called for a meeting of the fleet's captains and pilots the night before the ships were to sail again. As the men gathered in the *Trinidad*'s small cabin, Magellan realized the three captains might be setting a trap for him. Sure enough, they began arguing with Magellan about everything.

Cartagena insisted that he, not Magellan, should act as leader during the meeting. The others complained about the division of supplies and the route toward the west. Mendoza, in particular, demanded that the fleet sail southwest instead of south, as Magellan had planned. To their surprise, Magellan gave in to all of their demands.

The Spanish captains sailed with the fleet southward to another harbor on Tenerife to gather more supplies. At midnight, on October 3, 1519, the *Trinidad* led the other ships out of the Tenerife harbor and into the Atlantic. Magellan plotted a southwesterly course, just as the Spanish captains wanted.

Ferdinand Magellan

The peak of Tenerife, one of the Canary Islands

On the second day at sea, however, the *Trinidad* suddenly changed direction. It sailed more to the south as Magellan had originally planned. Cartagena ordered the *San Antonio* to sail close to the *Trinidad.*

Cartagena shouted across the waves, "Why have you changed course?"

"You will follow my lead and make no complaints," came Magellan's sharp reply.

With perhaps a hundred feet (thirty meters) of ocean between them, Cartagena could only glare angrily at Magellan. The three ships commanded by the Spanish captains fell meekly in line behind the *Trinidad.*

Magellan had shown his authority and avoided an ambush. King Manuel had sent a group of warships into the Atlantic to await Magellan's fleet. Had the captain-general sailed southwest, he would have fallen into the Portuguese trap.

Instead, the fleet continued its southward journey, hugging the coast of Africa. Pigafetta noted that many sharks with "terrible teeth" were spotted alongside the ships. He wrote that many were caught with iron hooks and added, probably from experience, that they were not good to eat. On October 18, a terrible storm struck the fleet, pounding it without mercy.

As the furious winds died down, the sailors aboard the *Trinidad* saw one of the most eerie sights faced by early seamen: St. Elmo's fire. Today, we know that St. Elmo's fire is actually the glow of atmospheric electricity around the mast of a ship. To these sailors at night, the star-shaped glow seemed to be the heavenly presence of St. Elmo, special protector of sailors. "When the blessed light was about to leave us," Pigafetta wrote, "so dazzling was the brightness that it cast into our eyes, that we all remained for more than an eighth of an hour blinded and calling for mercy."

St. Elmo's fire glowing from a ship's masthead

A ship becalmed in the doldrums of the Atlantic Ocean

A few days after the storm, the winds died down completely. Magellan had steered his fleet into an area known today as the doldrums. Here the winds are almost totally calm. He knew that King Manuel's warships would not look for his fleet there. But his clever move had a price. For three long weeks the entire fleet was becalmed, drifting lazily with the ocean currents. Worried that supplies were running low, Magellan was forced to cut each man's daily ration of food, water, and wine.

Ocean currents finally carried the fleet out of the doldrums. Wind once again filled the sails, and the ships at last began moving southwest across the Atlantic. The fleet crossed the equator around November 20, 1519, two months after leaving Spain. Pigafetta noted that they could no longer see the North Star. Ships' navigators would now have to steer by the Southern Cross, a constellation unknown to earlier Europeans.

A few days after the ships crossed the equator, the Spanish captains tried again to murder their leader. Magellan, the three Spanish captains, and Juan Rodríguez Serrano, the fifth captain of the fleet, met alone in the cabin of the *Trinidad*. The Spaniards began to hurl insults at Magellan, but he refused to argue.

Finally, Cartagena decided to make Magellan fight. He shouted that he would no longer follow Magellan's stupid commands.

This was a big mistake. Refusing to follow the leader's orders was a clear act of mutiny. The Spaniard, hoping to trap the captain-general, had fallen into Magellan's trap. At Magellan's signal, armed guards moved swiftly into the cabin. Cartagena drew his knife and called for the other two captains to fight. It was too late; they were hopelessly outnumbered. Magellan accused Cartagena of trying to start a mutiny; there were plenty of witnesses to back him up.

Cartagena was imprisoned aboard the *Victoria* and was relieved as captain of the *San Antonio*. His command, with a formal ceremony and a trumpet fanfare, was given to another Spaniard, Antonio de Coca.

The fleet now made good time crossing the South Atlantic. On December 6, a lookout spotted a shorebird and two days later sighted land. The sailors must have been eager to go ashore. More than two months had passed since they had taken fresh food and water on board. Many of the crew were already suffering from the early stages of scurvy.

To the sailors' dismay, Magellan refused to allow the ships to sail near the shore. He had good reasons for his decision. The fleet was in Portuguese waters off the coast of Brazil. Spain's King Charles had given strict orders not to go into Portuguese territory.

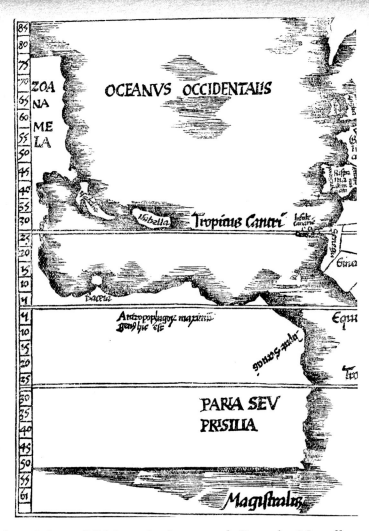

A map of part of the New World, drawn in the style of Ptolemy and published in 1515

Also, John of Lisbon had warned Captain Magellan about dangerous reefs along the coast. A ship caught on a reef could be pounded to splinters by the powerful Atlantic surf. Magellan was also aware that the vengeful King Manuel might have ships, or even soldiers on land, waiting to ambush his fleet.

For days, with land so close by, Magellan continued sailing southward along the coast of Brazil. John had told him about a great natural harbor to the south, beyond all Portuguese settlements. Urging his fellow sailors to be patient, Magellan steered a course to the harbor and reached it on December 13, 1519.

Above: A drawing of the entry to Rio de Janeiro harbor. Below: Sugar Loaf Mountain as it appears today

After nearly three months at sea, the fleet anchored in one of the most beautiful harbors in the world. Known today as Rio de Janeiro, it is the most famous vacation spot on the South American continent. Imposing mountains such as the now-famous Sugar Loaf Mountain and deep-green forests broken by fields of colorful wildflowers rose beyond the shoreline of the sky-blue ocean. When Magellan's fleet arrived in Rio de Janeiro, the sight must have been breathtaking.

No sooner had the ships dropped anchor than they were surrounded by canoes, each paddled by as many as forty South American natives. The Indians, members of the Guarani tribe, had never seen Europeans. The fleet arrived soon after a rain that had ended a severe drought. The Guarani believed that the Europeans, and even their ships, were gods. Perhaps these strange-looking men had sent the rain.

It was fortunate they thought so highly of Magellan and his crew. As Pigafetta pointed out, the Guarani were cannibals. "They eat the human flesh of their enemies," he wrote, "not because it is good, but because it is a certain established custom." Instead of trying to eat their European visitors, the Guarani became friends with them. For trinkets such as mirrors, combs, and bracelets, the Indians traded food and exotic animals such as parrots and monkeys.

South American parrot

For the tired sailors, weakened by scurvy, Rio de Janeiro must have seemed like paradise. All types of fresh fruits and vegetables were available that, unknown to anyone at the time, provided the vitamin C to cure scurvy. The Guarani made the voyagers feel welcome, even building them a house.

There was a great deal of work to be done to make the ships ready for the next leg of the voyage. Each ship had to be beached and turned over so its hull could be cleaned and rotted timbers replaced. The hulls then had to be painted with a coat of protective animal fat. Water casks had to be scoured clean and refilled with fresh water. Meat needed to be cured and dried to preserve it for the journey. There were many other tasks that called for backbreaking work.

It was no surprise that the sailors wanted to visit with the friendly Guarani Indians instead of work on the ships. Many of the sailors disobeyed Magellan's orders so they could spend more time on the mainland. Even Duarte Barbosa, Magellan's friend and relative, found the captain's orders too hard to follow. He deserted the *Trinidad* entirely for three days and nights. After begging Duarte to return, Magellan finally had to arrest him. He placed Duarte in irons until he accepted his responsibilities.

More trouble arose almost at once. Antonio de Coca, the new captain of the *San Antonio*, suddenly decided to set free the mutinous ex-captain Juan de Cartagena. Together they tried to take control of the fleet. Men loyal to Magellan stopped them before they could get too far. The captain-general was remarkably easy on the two. His only action was to take away Antonio de Coca's command and replace him with Alvaro de Mesquita, an uninspiring leader but a loyal sailor.

On Christmas Eve, 1519, the five ships were ready to sail again. They left the harbor on Christmas morning to explore the coast farther south. Dozens of Guarani followed, begging them to return. If another drought should strike, who would send the rain?

With the wind at their backs, the five Spanish ships sailed rapidly down the coast. On January 11, 1520, Magellan caught sight of three south-facing hills. John of Lisbon believed that these hills marked the opening of a great passage through the continent. Magellan was overjoyed. He had found *el paso*!

The captain-general ordered the *Santiago* to explore *el paso*. He found it hard to wait for the ship's return. A few days later, the *Santiago* sailed into view, but the crew brought Magellan bad news. John of Lisbon's passage was simply a river leading deeper into the continent. At first Magellan refused to believe it.

Aboard the *Trinidad*, he led the fleet westward through the passage. The ships moved slowly because of the light, changeable winds and increasingly shallow water. Finally, Magellan had one of the crew dip a bucket into the water. When it was hauled back on board, the captain-general drank from the bucket. He was deeply disappointed to find that it was not salt water but the sweet fresh water found in inland rivers.

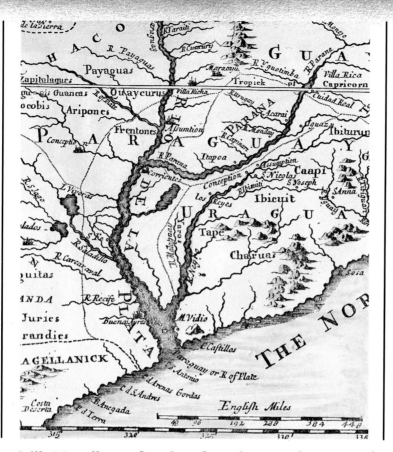

The Río de la Plata and surrounding country, from a map published in 1698

Still, Magellan refused to face the unwelcome truth. He ordered the men to use the fleet's five lifeboats to inspect every inch of both banks. He was certain that somewhere they would find salt water and a passage westward. After nearly three weeks, the captain-general finally had to admit this was no *el paso* after all.

A modern map of South America shows clearly that Magellan had discovered the Río de la Plata, or Silver River. This is a huge bay formed by two other rivers, and it separates present-day Argentina from Uruguay. It does not offer passage through South America.

Magellan's friend John of Lisbon had been wrong, and earlier maps and globes were incorrect. *El paso*, the magnet that attracted the entire expedition to this far-away wilderness, was not where they had thought it to be. Who knew if it even existed at all?

Chapter 6
El Paso:
The Strait of Magellan

When it was clear that the bay was not *el paso*, most of the men wanted to go no farther. But Magellan urged them to keep sailing south. He believed that somewhere along the coast they would find a route through the continent. The others were not so sure.

The Spanish captains called for a meeting of the entire crew on February 2, 1520. There, most of the sailors voted to return to Rio de Janeiro to spend the winter. In the Southern Hemisphere, winter was still several months away.

Magellan tried to persuade his men to press on southward. He pointed out that land to the north had been given to Portugal according to the Treaty of Tordesillas. Wintering in Rio de Janeiro could be regarded by Portugal as an act of war.

Also, *el paso* must be near. They had already sailed as far south as the southern tip of Africa. Magellan's argument must have sounded reasonable to the European sailors. At that time, everyone believed that the land masses of the Old World and the New World were about the same size.

Magellan urged his men to think about the warm climate and friendly natives of the Spice Islands, which were surely only a short distance beyond *el paso*.

Magellan's pleas won the men over. When the sun rose on February 3, 1520, the five ships left Río de la Plata and headed south.

For two chilly months the fleet fought its way southward against stiffening headwinds. They explored every bay, every inlet, every bend in the coastline in the search for *el paso*. These coastal waters, even today, are regarded as among the most dangerous in the world. During winter, ships avoid them whenever possible. Many times during the hazardous voyage, the ships became separated. The *Victoria* ran aground on a sandbar and was lucky to escape unharmed. In a tremendous gale, the mast of the *Santiago* was broken and had to be repaired. The *San Antonio* began leaking badly.

An artist's concept of the horrors lurking in the dangerous waters off the South American coast

Icebergs looming in the treacherous seas near Antarctica

As they drew nearer to Antarctica and the winter months, cold and ice became more severe. Head winds blew like icy hurricanes, sometimes pushing the ships farther back in a day than they had sailed since morning. Day after day, the sailors were drenched by huge Atlantic waves that seemed to reach the sky. Their clothes became as brittle as ice in the bitterly cold air. More often now, the sailors spotted icebergs that could have ripped through the hull of a ship as if it were paper. Only the brilliant sailing of Captain Magellan saved the fleet from destruction.

By the middle of March, even Magellan realized he could sail no farther. For two weeks, he searched for a safe harbor to spend the winter. Finally, on March 31, 1520, a suitable spot was found on the south coast of what is now Argentina. The natural harbor was cold, dark, and deserted. Yet it offered a safe haven from the pounding surf of the Atlantic. Magellan named the fleet's winter home San Julián, still its name today.

As soon as the fleet had anchored, Magellan spotted small boats scurrying back and forth between the *Concepción* and the *Victoria*. It wasn't hard to guess the reason. The Spanish captains did not like the idea of wintering in the frozen San Julián wilderness. They were planning a mutiny.

The next day Magellan announced that, because of the long winter ahead, he would have to cut each man's daily ration of biscuits and wine by half. Crewmen and officers complained bitterly. Magellan suggested that five sailors from each ship meet on the *Trinidad* to talk over their grievances. At the meeting, he reminded the

Marino Glacier on Argentina's Patagonian coast

men of the bravery of Portuguese sailors who had sailed around Africa with Vasco da Gama. He pointed to the pleasures that awaited them in the Spice Islands in spring. Once again, the captain-general was able to calm their fears.

A similar meeting between Magellan and the captains and pilots of the fleet did not go as well. Most of the officers wanted to leave the harbor at once and head north toward warmer waters. Magellan refused to change his plan, and the meeting ended in anger.

On the morning of Easter Sunday, some of the crew attended a Mass at a makeshift altar on the mainland. Although Magellan and his aides expected violence and came fully armed, the service went peacefully. That night, however, the mutiny began.

The Spanish captains first tried to capture the *San Antonio*. On that ship Magellan had replaced not one but two Spanish captains—Juan de Cartagena, followed by Antonio de Coca. The ship's third captain, Alvaro de Mesquita, was loyal to Magellan.

A little before midnight, thirty armed men in the *Concepción*'s lifeboat rowed silently to the *San Antonio*. They were led by Cartagena, Coca, and Captain Quesada from the *Concepción*, accompanied by one of his officers, Juan Sebastián. When they reached the *San Antonio*, they waited while one of the sailors lowered a rope ladder. Quietly, they climbed on board.

Within minutes, the intruders had captured Captain Mesquita and locked him in chains. One of the *San Antonio*'s officers realized what was happening and tried to shout a warning. Quesada drew his knife and stabbed the man repeatedly. Sailors loyal to Magellan, most of whom had been sleeping, could do little to fight the mutineers. Most were imprisoned in the ship's hold.

Mutinous crewmen wave to Captain Mesquita as he is dragged below deck and locked in chains.

At this point, the intruders had control of the *Concepción*, the *Victoria*, and now the *San Antonio*. Under cover of darkness, they should have been able to attack and overcome the *Trinidad* and the little *Santiago*. But they faced a serious problem.

The rebellious Spanish captains, and many of their officers in on the mutiny, were not really sailors. Most had been given their rank in the expedition because they were wealthy and knew how to flatter princes and clergymen. Many of the skilled sailors, who remained loyal to Magellan, had been imprisoned by the mutineers. They were unable and unwilling to help launch a naval attack against the *Trinidad* and the *Santiago*.

The three rebel ships remained at anchor until the next morning, April 2, 1520. Magellan quickly learned what had happened. He ordered his loyal sailors to arms and loaded the cannons aboard his two remaining ships. After exchanging written notes with the rebel captains gathered aboard the *San Antonio*, he waited for the mutineers' next move.

Toward midday, the *San Antonio*'s lifeboat, loaded with sailors, began rowing toward the *Concepción*. Before it could reach the ship, the small boat was caught in a powerful Atlantic current. It was pulled toward the pounding breakers at the mouth of the harbor. As the swirling current pushed the lifeboat near the *Trinidad*, the frightened sailors began crying for help. One of Magellan's men threw them a rope. After a fierce battle with the current, Magellan's crew managed to pull the boat to the *Trinidad*.

Once they were aboard the ship, Magellan saw that the luckless boatmen were common sailors, with no officers among them. He gave each one a friendly greeting and a hearty drink of wine. The sailors in turn told him everything they knew about the rebellion.

Soon, Magellan had developed a plan to put down the mutiny. He ordered the rescued sailors to change clothes with some of his own men. The first part of a clever trap was about to be sprung.

The loyal sailors, dressed in the mutineers' clothes, crowded into the *San Antonio*'s lifeboat. Following Magellan's orders, they started rowing slowly past the *Victoria*. Meanwhile, Magellan sent a second boat with three apparently unarmed sailors also toward the *Victoria*. One of the men shouted that he had a letter for Captain Mendoza and was allowed on board.

But soon as he reached Mendoza's cabin, the man pulled out his dagger and stabbed the captain to death. At a signal, Magellan's disguised sailors rowed swiftly for the *Victoria*, boarded it, and seized control.

With the *Victoria* recaptured, Magellan was ready to spring the second part of his trap. He ordered the anchors raised on the three ships now under his control. The vessels drifted, almost unnoticed, toward the mouth of the harbor. Before the two remaining Spanish captains knew what was happening, Magellan's ships had blocked the harbor entrance. Quesada decided to abandon Cartagena and tried to run the *San Antonio* through the blockade. Instead, he was quickly captured by a group of men from the *Trinidad* led by Magellan. When Cartagena saw Quesada's capture, he gave up and begged for mercy.

Captain-General Magellan had put down the mutiny with a loss of only one life, that of the rebel Captain Mendoza. Even after a five-day trial that found the mutineers guilty, Magellan showed unusual mercy. Just one man was executed, Captain Gaspar de Quesada, who had brutally stabbed an officer aboard the *San Antonio*. The officer suffered for two months before he died.

Magellan knew that Juan de Cartagena had political power back in Spain. He merely locked the Spanish captain in a cabin of one of the ships. From this comfortable prison, however, Cartagena and a Spanish priest plotted yet another mutiny. They were caught and court-martialed again. For punishment, Magellan had the pair marooned. They were put off the ships and would have to fend for themselves in the wilderness. The remaining mutineers were forced to work in chains cleaning and repairing the fleet. At the end of winter, all were pardoned and allowed to return to their posts.

The mutiny was a grim way to begin the hard winter. But more bad news was to follow. To make it through the cold months ahead, they would have to dig into the ship's supplies. Magellan soon discovered that nearly half of the provisions were missing. Portuguese spies had stolen them while the fleet was still in Spain. Magellan ordered some of the sailors to fish and hunt for food.

In his diary, Antonio Pigafetta gives a short and somewhat confused account of the mutiny and other events during the winter at San Julián. King Charles or one of the court officials may have forced him to change what he had written. Perhaps they did not want others to know how badly the Spanish captains had acted.

Ships tossed on the waves.

Penguins, described by Pigafetta as looking like geese with black feathers

The South American llama was a strange sight to Magellan's crew.

However, Pigafetta wrote in detail about the mysteries of the land they explored. He described animals that seemed bizarre to the Europeans, including penguins and llamas. Penguins, he wrote, looked like geese with black feathers. Llamas had "a head and ears as large as those of a mule, a neck and body like those of a camel, the legs of a deer, and the tail of a horse."

Pigafetta also wrote about one of the oddest events of Magellan's long voyage. He began with the early months at the port of San Julián.

"We passed two months in that place without seeing anyone. One day we suddenly saw a naked man of giant stature on the shore of the port, dancing, singing, and throwing dust on his head. The captain-general sent one of our men to the giant so that he might perform the same actions as a sign of peace. Having done that, the man led the giant to an islet into the presence of the captain-general. When the giant was in the captain-general's and our presence, he marveled greatly, and made signs with one finger raised upward, believing that we had come from the sky. He was so tall that we reached only to his waist, and he was well proportioned."

Soon they saw other giants, including women. Magellan named them Patagonians, meaning big feet. For a time, the Europeans and the Patagonians got along well. Then the crew tried to capture one to take back home and trouble broke out. One of the sailors was killed and a Patagonian was wounded. After that, the giants regarded the Europeans as enemies, threatening them often.

Patagonians hunting with the bola, a stone tied to the end of a leather thong that is thrown around the neck or legs of the hunted animal. The bola is still used in Argentina today.

Quoniambec, one of the natives Magellan and his men encountered on their voyage

Curiously, today the natives of that area of South America are short. Yet other early explorers, including Francis Drake of England, reported seeing giants more than seven feet (two meters) tall. If they ever really existed, the Patagonians disappeared many years ago. Even today, however, the southern tip of Argentina is called Patagonia. Magellan's name for this land of mysterious giants has survived more than four-and-a-half centuries.

Magellan feared that the Patagonians might attack. He sent his most skilled captain, Juan Rodríguez Serrano, on a desperate mission in the dead of winter. Leaving San Julián in mid-July, Serrano sailed the *Santiago* south seeking *el paso*, or at least a safer harbor.

He found a harbor at a river he named Río de Santa Cruz about sixty miles south of San Julián. After exploring the place for some time, Serrano headed back northward. But the *Santiago* was caught in violent winds and waves and was destroyed. All but one of the crew managed to escape to shore.

Magellan himself sailed to rescue the stranded sailors. After seeing the fine harbor, he decided the fleet would stay there for the rest of the winter.

As the days grew warmer and longer, the fleet prepared to set sail once again. By this time, even many of Magellan's most loyal followers wanted to give up the search for *el paso*.

The captain-general admitted to the crew that he was not exactly sure where the passage lay. Yet he insisted that they continue south to a point where they would be stopped by polar ice. Somehow, despite the hardships, he persuaded them to agree.

Juan Serrano, who had lost the *Santiago*, was put in charge of the *Concepción*. Duarte Barbosa was made captain of the *Victoria*. Magellan and Alvaro de Mesquita remained in command of the *Trinidad* and the *San Antonio*. As the next leg of the voyage began, all the ships were commanded by captains loyal to Magellan.

With the *Trinidad* in the lead, the four ships sailed out of Río de Santa Cruz on October 18, 1520. They were met by a brutal storm blowing off the Antarctic wastelands. After two days, the fleet sailed beyond a sharp point of land where the sailors spotted a wide, shallow bay leading inland. Against the advice of most of his men, Magellan decided to send the *San Antonio* and the *Concepción* to explore the inlet. As soon as the two ships started off, another violent storm blew in from the south.

For two days, the *Trinidad* and the *Victoria* tried to stay afloat in pounding surf and howling gales. When calm at last returned, the *San Antonio* and the *Concepción* were nowhere to be seen. Fearing the ships were lost, Magellan headed after them through the bay. Although the land was barren and looked unpopulated, the voyagers could see columns of smoke rising in the distance. They quickly forgot the smoke when a lookout spotted two ships sailing rapidly toward them.

The *San Antonio* and the *Concepción* had returned. Their crews were jumping up and down on decks, yelling and screaming with excitement. When he heard their report, Magellan was filled with joy and relief. The two ships had followed the bay into a narrow passage. It opened up into a wide inland bay stretching west as far as the eye could see. When they crossed the great bay, they entered another narrow passage. This channel contained salt water and its level rose and fell just like ocean tides. It was no river, the men proclaimed. *El paso* at long last had been found!

Even at this joyous moment, many of his Spanish officers still wanted to turn back. They urged Magellan to sail east across the familiar Atlantic Ocean to the Spice Islands. Once again, Magellan convinced the men to go on.

Sailing in single file, the fleet entered the narrow ocean passage that flowed between huge rock cliffs. Soon after the strait widened into a bay, the explorers saw the huge body of a dead whale on the beach. Some of the men went ashore and, three miles inland, found the bodies of several Patagonian giants. They had been placed on platforms raised above the ground on sticks. It looked like a tribal burial ground.

The fleet continued to sail south and west through the inland bay until they sighted a large island. Captain

Magellan ordered the *San Antonio* to explore one side of the island while the remaining ships sailed along the shore. Magellan led the rest of the fleet across the bay until nightfall. They anchored at a stream Magellan named the River of Sardines. On October 31, while some of his men fished for sardines, he sent Gonzalo Gómez de Espinosa with a small crew in the *Trinidad*'s lifeboat to explore deeper into the strait.

After four days, Espinosa returned in triumph. He had followed the strait all the way to a great sea. Although he reported the waters ahead were rough, the way to the Spice Islands was now clear. Magellan urged his crew to hunt and fish for more food for the final leg of the journey. There was little else to do, since they were still waiting for the *San Antonio* to rejoin the fleet.

Mount Sarmiento, the highest point of Tierra del Fuego at the southern tip of South America

A nineteenth-century illustration of the Strait of Magellan

A full week went by and the *San Antonio* still did not return. Magellan led search parties clear back to the Atlantic looking for the missing ship. He finally realized that the *San Antonio*'s third captain, Alvaro de Mesquita, had decided to return to Spain.

Magellan sailed back to the River of Sardines and took stock of the food on board the three remaining ships. The provisions were pitifully small. Much had been carried away on the *San Antonio*. Magellan would have to sail an uncharted ocean with dangerously low supplies. He told his men to double their efforts hunting game and catching fish.

The next day, the Europeans were surprised to see six Indians, along with three children, paddling through the strait in a well-constructed bark canoe. The Indians were even more surprised to see the tall European ships.

They began bowing deeply in their canoe, as if they were praying to gods. Through sign language, the Europeans and the South American Indians could speak to one another. The Indians came aboard the *Trinidad*, ate a hearty meal, and continued talking, mostly through sign language. It turned out that the natives knew the Patagonian giants well and were afraid of them.

When night fell, the visitors simply lay down on the deck of the *Trinidad* and went to sleep. The sailors tried to keep watch over them all night. But by morning the Indians, along with their fine canoe, had disappeared. Many sailors believed that the mysterious visitors had not been people at all but spirits from another world.

Above: Indians stripping bark from trees to construct bark canoes

Left: Pigafetta's map of the southern end of South America. North is at the bottom and south is at the top. The Strait of Magellan is the passage of water near the top of the map, with the Pacific Ocean on the right.

Magellan discovers the passage between the Atlantic and the Pacific oceans. Although he named it the Strait of All Saints, it is called the Strait of Magellan in his honor.

On November 24, 1520, the fleet of three ships left the River of Sardines and headed toward the unknown ocean. By nightfall, howling winds and rushing tides made it impossible to anchor the ships. During the two nights they spent in the narrow strait, Magellan and his crew saw countless fires from Indian camps. The captain named the land *Tierra de los Fuegos*, or land of fires.

This desolate region is still known by the slightly shortened name of Tierra del Fuego. It is really a group of islands, through which Magellan's ships sailed. Englishman Francis Drake rounded the islands' southernmost point in 1578.

Magellan also named the passage he discovered the Strait of All Saints. Today, however, it is called the Strait of Magellan in honor of the courageous explorer.

When the fleet finally arrived at the unknown sea, the voyagers all believed that the Orient and the Spice Islands were only a short distance away. They had no idea that the world's largest body of water—the Pacific Ocean—stretched out before them. Eventually, Magellan would also name this great sea.

An early map of the Strait of Magellan. Notice the penguin in the lower right-hand corner.

Chapter 7
The Endless Pacific

On Wednesday, November 28, 1520, Ferdinand Magellan and his three remaining ships were ready to strike out across the vast ocean. Beyond the choppy waters of the strait, the sea was blue and calm.

Before starting out, the sailors knelt down on the deck of the *Trinidad* while a priest led them in prayer. They sang a hymn and then each ship fired one of its cannon in honor of the historic moment.

Finally, Captain Magellan made a brief speech.

"Gentlemen," he said, "we are now entering waters in which no ship has sailed before. May they always remain as calm for us as they are this morning. In this great hope, I name the sea the *Mar Pacifico*." This is Spanish for "calm sea," and that sea is known today as the Pacific Ocean.

As soon as the fleet had moved away from the South American coast, Magellan began heading due north. The crew, used to warm Mediterranean waters, were eager to leave the chilly weather of the Southern Hemisphere.

Two South American natives traveled with Magellan. One was a Patagonian giant, brought on board when the fleet was still in San Julián. According to Pigafetta, the crew called him Paulo. The giant's name was entered into a logbook as Juan Gigante. There was also a Guarani Indian aboard who seems to have been a stowaway. Pigafetta spent a great deal of time with both South Americans and wrote the meanings of dozens of their words in his diary.

On the fifth day in the Pacific, the brisk head winds changed direction, pushing the fleet along faster. For days the ships continued north, often within sight of the western coast of South America. About three weeks after leaving the strait, Magellan changed course from north to northwest. According to the best maps Magellan owned, Asia should have been near. Although Asia was not yet in sight, the weather grew warmer. Most of the sailors began dreaming about the fortune each would make from the Spice Islands.

It may have been at this point during the voyage that Pigafetta wrote down his observations of the night sky in the Southern Hemisphere. "The Antarctic Pole is not so starry as the Arctic," he wrote. "Many small stars clustered together are seen, which have the appearance of two clouds of mist. There is but little distance between them, and they are somewhat dim." The "clouds of mist" that Pigafetta described can be seen only in the Southern Hemisphere near the equator. They are really distant galaxies made up of billions of stars. Modern astronomers call them the Magellanic Clouds.

As Magellan's voyage continued, tail winds sped the fleet on its way. The weather became even warmer, a delightful change from the almost constant cold of the previous months. Duties aboard ship were light. The

30 DOR

SN 1987a
REGION

sailors amused themselves relaxing on the decks and catching some of the strange fish they found in the Pacific. To keep them out of mischief, Magellan ordered daily battle drills for the crew. But as the days and nights passed, Magellan noticed many of the sailors were beginning to act lazy.

In fact, this was the first sign of scurvy. The condition of the food and water aboard the ships did not help matters. Under the hot sun, much of it spoiled and became filled with worms. The water turned putrid, and hardly anyone could drink it. Even the wine was gone.

Six weeks after leaving the Strait of Magellan, conditions were so bad that crewmen started dying. The Patagonian giant and the South American Indian were among the first victims of disease and malnutrition. The sailors' health grew worse each day. By the middle of January 1521, one-third of the crew was unable to walk.

A telescope's view of the large Magellanic cloud, which is a neighboring galaxy to our Milky Way. Magellan and his crew were the first Europeans to view these clusters of stars.

An island of volcanic origin in the Pacific Ocean

Magellan threw aside the crude maps he had brought, realizing they were worthless in these waters. Many of the sailors feared that the world was not round after all. They would sail forever through an endless expanse of sea. But by January 24, the explorers found proof that they had not passed the end of the world.

An island appeared on the horizon. It wasn't much— merely a small circle of nearly barren land formed from the walls of a volcano whose crater lay below the water's surface. The uninhabited island, soon named San Pablo, was a welcome sight for the frightened sailors. Today San Pablo, 670 miles (1,078 kilometers) southwest of Mexico, is called Clipperton Island.

The fleet anchored off the tiny island for four days. Although there was no fresh water on San Pablo, the sailors spread out the ships' sails in a rainstorm and gathered clear drinking water. The island harbored an abundance of fresh food: fish, crabs, and seabirds whose nests were filled with eggs. Much of this food was devoured by the half-starved crew. They smoked more food and brought it aboard the three ships.

Unfortunately, no fruits or vegetables grew on the volcanic island. Without the vitamin C these foods would have provided, scurvy grew worse among the crew. Two weeks after leaving San Pablo, a lookout spotted another island, today called Clarion Island. As the ships drew closer, the men could see coconuts growing at the tops of palm trees. The thought of eating fresh coconut meat must have made their mouths water. More importantly, coconut contained the vitamin C that could quickly cure their scurvy.

The island of San Pablo, formed from the walls of a volcano whose crater lies underwater

At this point, however, Magellan made a serious mistake. The water around the little island was too deep for the ships to drop anchor. Wind and ocean currents quickly pushed the fleet beyond the island. To sail back against the wind would require plotting a long, triangular course that could take several days. Magellan, believing that the Orient was just over the horizon, decided to sail on. It was a tragic error in judgment.

Unknown to Magellan and the others, the fleet was nowhere near the Orient. In fact, the course that Magellan took in these unmapped waters turned out to be incredibly unlucky. Although the Pacific contains many groups of islands, the course he sailed missed all of them.

Now near the equator, the voyagers found their food and water spoiling quickly under the broiling sun. Pigafetta described their supplies. "We ate biscuit which was no longer biscuit, but powder of biscuit swarming with worms, for they had eaten the good. It stank strongly of the urine of rats. We drank yellow water that had been putrid for many days."

The horrible days of February 1521 passed, and conditions continued to get worse. Finally, all the food was gone. Some of the men caught rats and sold them to the highest bidder. Magellan scraped sawdust from the insides of empty food barrels to make a paste the men tried to eat. Parts of the ships' leather riggings were soaked in water for days and then eaten, or at least swallowed. Late in the month, Magellan changed course often, finally heading due west in a desperate search for land. Had he continued north a little longer, he would have discovered the Hawaiian Islands.

Pigafetta and Magellan were among the few sailors who were not seriously ill. When the ship's doctor died,

An artist's concept of some of the visions seen by starved and diseased seamen

Magellan took care of the sick. Most of the sailors became too weak to work. The captain-general began doing many of their jobs. Before long, the sailors did not have the strength to lower the sails at night or to raise them in the morning. The ships continued sailing at night, each captain praying that rocks or coral reefs were not ahead.

Many times a lookout, too weak to stand, would hoarsely cry out, "Land ho!" But the land turned out to be a cloud, a school of fish, or a mirage. The sailors were so sick they were seeing things. By the early days of March, even all the rats on the ships had been eaten.

By March 5, nineteen sailors had died from scurvy and starvation and had been buried at sea. Sharks began swimming behind the ships, following the trail of sea burials. Only one sailor on the *Trinidad* remained strong enough to climb the mast and look out over the ocean. When he came back down, he reported that he had seen a bank of clouds that looked like land. As evening fell, the breeze died, and the ships came to a near standstill. Most of the men decided it had been another mirage.

At dawn the next day, March 6, 1521, the same sailor managed to climb the mast again. As he looked out over the vast ocean, he could hardly believe his eyes. For some time he could not speak. A large landmass lay clearly in front of him. "Praise God!" he finally screamed. "Land! Land!"

The sailors on the deck below, some too weak to move, cheered loudly. The *Trinidad* fired its cannon and was soon answered by shots from the *Concepción* and the *Victoria*. Around midday, the men saw a second island, even closer than the first, and then a third. The *Trinidad* changed course for the largest island, but the wind died down and made progress slow. During the moonlit night, the ships barely moved. By dawn, however, the voyagers could see canoes and grass huts along the beaches of the nearest island.

Magellan knew they would be meeting unknown people. He ordered the few sailors who were strong enough to put on armor. As they neared the sandy beaches, it was clear that no one had the strength to lower the sails. Magellan ordered the ropes holding them up to be cut. The sails fell with a sound like thunder, and the ship dropped anchor. Magellan's fleet had reached the island today called Guam.

The weakened sailors struggled with the *Trinidad*'s lifeboat so that a small party could row to shore. Just as the boat dropped into the water, hundreds of islanders in large dugout canoes swarmed around the *Trinidad*. In a moment a war party had climbed onto the decks of the ship.

The healthy islanders came armed with clubs, spears, and shields decorated with human hair. When they saw the sick and exhausted Europeans, the islanders knew they could easily overpower the sailors.

The islanders began stripping the ship of every item that could be carried off, passing their booty down to others waiting in canoes below. The few Europeans who tried to stop them were scornfully thrown aside. Some sailors were still strong enough to fire their crossbows, however, and a half-dozen natives fell under a storm of arrows.

The islanders quickly jumped into their canoes and paddled to shore. They pulled the *Trinidad*'s empty lifeboat with them so they could not be followed. Plentiful supplies of food and fresh water were within sight, but Magellan dared not allow anyone on shore. All chances of peaceful bartering with the natives had been lost.

For another night the fleet of three ships moved out into the ocean. But at dawn the next morning, the starving Europeans prepared to land at any cost. The ships moved in close to the beach and fired their cannons directly into the native village, destroying a number of grass huts.

The islanders fled into the jungle. Magellan then led a landing party of about sixty men into the deserted village. The starving explorers began drinking fresh water from a nearby stream and devouring food left behind by the villagers.

The sailors gathered stores of coconuts, bananas, sweet potatoes, and other fruits and vegetables. The fresh food, along with hundreds of chickens and dozens of pigs, were carried onto the three ships. Magellan ordered his men to work quickly; it was a wise command. Soon after the ships raised their anchors and began sailing away, natives in dozens of war canoes followed them well out to sea.

Pigafetta described the scene. "Those people seeing us departing followed us with more than one hundred boats. . . . They approached the ships showing us fish, feigning that they would give them to us; but then threw stones at us and fled. . . . We saw some women in their boats who were crying out and tearing their hair, for love, I believe, of those whom we had killed." The natives continued to pelt the European fleet with stones and shake their spears. Captain Magellan must have thought another battle was about to begin, but he ordered no action taken. At last the canoes turned around and headed back to the island.

That night, the sailors ate their first hearty meal in months. Magellan knew the food would last only a few days, and they would need more for the rest of the voyage. He steered for the nearby island of Rota. When the fleet arrived, it was greeted by more natives in canoes. These boats kept their distance, however. The people had probably been warned about the European ships from the natives on Guam.

Eventually, Magellan was able to talk with the people on Rota. Without bloodshed, he traded knives and hatchets for fresh food and gave gifts to some of the officials from the island. No doubt he hoped to erase the bad impression his men had left after the bloody fight on Guam.

An old print of Ferdinand Magellan

One of the hundreds of tropical islands in the Pacific Ocean

The fleet left Rota on March 9 and sailed for a week, passing many small islands. On March 16, the ships came at last to a large island, probably Samar in the eastern Philippines. Unable to find a place to drop anchor, the fleet continued south. They finally stopped at an uninhabited little island nearby. There they built shelters for the sailors who were still sick. During the nine days the fleet remained on the island, most of the men recovered fully.

The expedition was visited by natives who traveled in canoes from neighboring islands. Through sign language, the natives explained that the islands were part of a vast chain stretching north and south for hundreds of miles. Many of the sailors were excited to see that an island chief wore jewelry decorated with gold.

Rowing ashore from the mother ship

With the crew in good health and high spirits once again, the fleet set sail on March 25, 1521, heading southwest. The ships passed a number of other islands but did not stop. One night, while resting at anchor, they saw a bonfire on a small island to the north. At dawn on March 28, the ships sailed toward the little island where they had seen the fire. As they reached land, a canoe carrying eight islanders approached the ships, keeping a careful distance.

Henry of Malacca, Magellan's slave, called out to the islanders in the Malayan tongue. The men in the canoe answered him in Malayan! Here, for the first time in the 550-day voyage, was proof that the fleet had reached the Orient. The Malay Peninsula, which Magellan had visited in 1509, could not be far away.

The islanders in the canoe refused to come near any of the larger European ships. In his diary, Pigafetta recorded Captain Magellan's efforts to greet them:

"The captain, seeing that they would not trust us, threw them out a red cap and other things tied to a bit of wood. They received them very gladly and went away quickly to advise their king. About two hours later we saw two *balanghai* coming. They are large boats and are so called by these people. They were full of men, and their king was in the larger of them, being seated under an awning of mats. When the king came near the flagship, the slave spoke to him. The king understood him, for in those districts the kings know more languages than the other people. He ordered some of his men to enter the ships, but he always remained in his *balanghai*, at some little distance from the ship, until his own men returned; and as soon as they returned he departed. The captain-general showed great honor to the men who entered the ship, and gave them some presents, for which the king wished before his departure to give the captain a large bar of gold and basketful of ginger. The latter, however, thanked the king heartily but would not accept it. In the afternoon, we went in the ships and anchored near the dwellings of the king."

The king described by Pigafetta was Rajah Colambu. The rajah ruled the small Philippine island called Limassawa.

On the next day, March 29, Magellan persuaded the rajah to come aboard the *Trinidad*. With Henry of Malacca acting as interpreter, Magellan and the island king quickly became friends. They tasted a drop of each other's blood, a gesture that made them blood brothers. Even when trouble came later, the two men remained loyal friends.

Magellan landing at Cebu in the Philippine Islands

The Spanish fleet remained anchored at Limassawa for a week. During that time, which included the Christian holy days of Good Friday and Easter, the priests held several Masses on the island. Many of the natives had no formal religion of their own. They liked these ceremonies and wanted to become Christians too.

While the Europeans were on the island, many sailors helped to harvest the island's rice crop. They enjoyed the colorful harvest festival. They also began to trade for gold. Some of the natives were willing to exchange their gold nuggets for equal weights of iron.

In the meantime, Magellan learned from Rajah Colambu about a large island called Cebu, just a few days away by boat. The people of Cebu, according to the rajah, were very wealthy.

By now the Spanish captains were impatient to sail the short distance to the Spice Islands. Magellan, however, was eager to explore more of the Philippines, having already claimed them for Spain. Once again, Magellan won the argument. Escorted by Rajah Colambu and some islanders, the Spanish fleet sailed for Cebu on April 3, 1521.

They reached the island four days later. Along much of the coast, large houses built on stilts stood at the water's edge. As the fleet sailed into the harbor, more than a thousand canoes, many with bright cotton sails, followed the ships in a gala harbor parade. Magellan came ashore to pay his respects to the powerful rajah of Cebu.

Native dwellings in New Guinea in the South Pacific Ocean

For the first time in more than a year, the captain-general met a worldly and educated ruler. The rajah of Cebu had Chinese and Arab advisers by his side. From them, he had learned about the cruel attacks by Portuguese fleets on cities in Africa and Asia. He may have wished to avoid a fight with these newly arrived Europeans. Their ships carried more firepower than any others in the East.

So the rajah allowed a brisk trade to spring up between the Europeans and his island subjects. Many wanted to exchange food and gold for mirrors, combs, scissors, and other trinkets. Soon the Filipinos and the Europeans became friends—or so it seemed.

This "friendship" was not to last for long. As in many voyages of exploration at the time, Europeans felt that they were better than the native peoples they encountered. They felt they had the right to impose their customs and beliefs on the natives. Some Europeans truly believed they were improving the natives' way of life. Others, however, were simply seeking wealth, power, or glory. In many cases, the natives fought back. Some succeeded, but most did not.

One day, the rajah of Cebu told Magellan that he would like to become a Christian. Magellan, a very religious man, was happy to hear the news. Now that Spain claimed the Philippine Islands, the captain-general wanted to save as many souls as he could. On Sunday, April 14, 1521, a great ceremony was held on Cebu. In front of a rough, wooden cross, the rajah and his family were baptized in the Christian faith.

Many other natives followed their king's lead. According to Pigafetta, "five hundred men were baptized before mass." In the days that followed, news of the great ceremony spread throughout many other islands.

Over the next two weeks, thousands of natives, including many chiefs, were baptized as well. For Magellan, it was a time of great happiness.

But the Spanish captains were angry at the delay these ceremonies caused. If they were ever to reach the Spice Islands, they had to find some way to stop Magellan.

They decided to ask the rajah of Cebu for help. As part of a carefully planned trap, the rajah told Magellan that some chiefs on nearby islands scorned Christianity. He said they also refused to swear obedience to the king of Spain, as the rajahs of Limassawa and Cebu had done.

At this point, Magellan, usually so sensible and cautious, seems to have lost his head. He sent a force of armed sailors to attack one of the most powerful of the island chiefs, Cacique Cilapulapu. The chief ruled on the island of Mactan, east of Cebu across a narrow channel. Magellan's force burned the chief's village and massacred many of his soldiers. Despite this victory, the rajah of Cebu told Magellan that the chief still refused to surrender.

On April 26, Magellan asked for volunteers for a landing party to capture Cilapulapu. The Spanish officers openly laughed at him, and fewer than sixty common sailors and servants stepped forward. His blood brother Rajah Colambu offered to give him a force of a thousand native warriors, but Magellan refused.

"God will protect my men," he said.

After waiting offshore for hours, the pitifully small attack force under Magellan's command landed on Mactan early on April 27, 1521. The Europeans were quickly driven back by a large force of natives. While Magellan and a small group fought the enemy, the rest of his men retreated to the sea and rowed back to the Spanish fleet.

Magellan was killed on April 27, 1521, during his foolhardy attack on the natives of Mactan. He never lived to receive credit for planning and embarking on the first voyage around the globe.

According to Pigafetta, who fought at Magellan's side, the tiny band of Europeans held off thousands of natives for more than an hour. Offshore, the Spanish fleet did nothing. Rajah Colambu rowed his canoe from ship to ship, begging the Spanish officers to help in the fight. They laughingly insisted it was Magellan's battle, not theirs. Colambu brought his canoes close to shore, hoping to pick up survivors. At that point, the cannons of the Spanish ships opened fire. But instead of shooting at the natives, the Spaniards fired at Colambu's rescue party! The little boats were sunk, and ten of Colambu's men were killed.

Moments later, Ferdinand Magellan lay dead in the shallow ocean water, killed by native spears. As if waiting for that very moment, the Spanish officers sent the fleet's lifeboats ashore to pick up survivors, including Pigafetta. Magellan's body was left on the beach.

Magellan had fallen victim to his own religious fervor and devotion to the king of Spain. The voyage he had led so far and through so many hardships was unfinished.

Yet even in his death he had achieved an astonishing feat. The Philippine Islands, on whose shores his lifeless body finally rested, may have been familiar to Magellan. He may have reached the Philippines in 1512 when he sailed east from the Malay Peninsula for Portugal. In 1521 he had reached them again by sailing west for Spain. He and his slave Henry of Malacca were the first people in history to travel completely around the world.

The coat-of-arms of Ferdinand Magellan

Chapter 8
The Voyage after Magellan

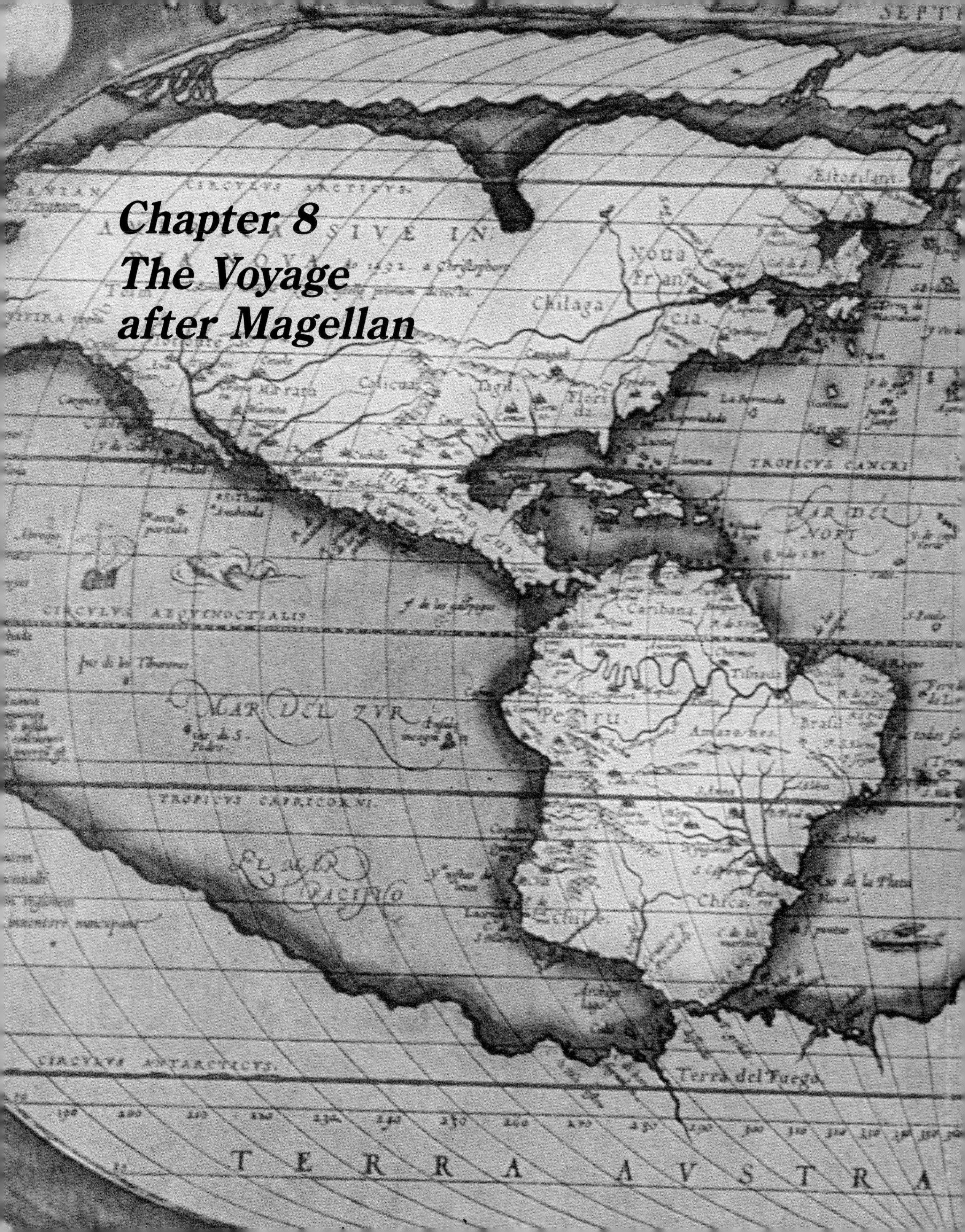

In his diary, Pigafetta summed up his feelings about Captain Magellan: "Among the other virtues which he possessed, he was more constant than ever any one else in the greatest of adversity. He endured hunger better than all the others, and more accurately than any man in the world did he understand sea charts and navigation. And that this was the truth was seen openly, for no other had had so much natural talent nor the boldness to learn how to circumnavigate the world, as he had almost done."

The Spanish officers who had done nothing to save Magellan soon paid for their action. Duarte Barbosa became the fleet commander, but neither he nor anyone else knew how to lead the Europeans safely home.

The Spaniards tried to organize meetings with many of the Philippine rajahs and chiefs. They were foolish enough to use Henry of Malacca as messenger and translator to help them. Henry, angry at their role in his master's death, arranged with the other chiefs to set a trap for the captains. The chiefs told the Spaniards that they wanted to send precious jewels to the king of Spain. When the officers went ashore to collect the gems, many of them were slaughtered. Barbosa and Juan Serrano were captured and probably killed.

João Lopes Carvalho then took command as captain-general of the fleet. Of the 241 men who had sailed from Spain, only about 115 remained alive, not enough to man the three ships. Therefore, the new commander ordered the *Concepción* burned. Just before the ship was set ablaze, Carvalho ordered all of Magellan's personal papers placed on board the *Concepción*. The Spanish captain did not want any record of the San Julián mutiny to survive.

On May 1, 1521, the *Trinidad* and the *Victoria* sailed from Cebu. In the months that followed, the men aboard the ships showed their true characters. Under

European merchant ships among an array of Oriental vessels in a Chinese harbor

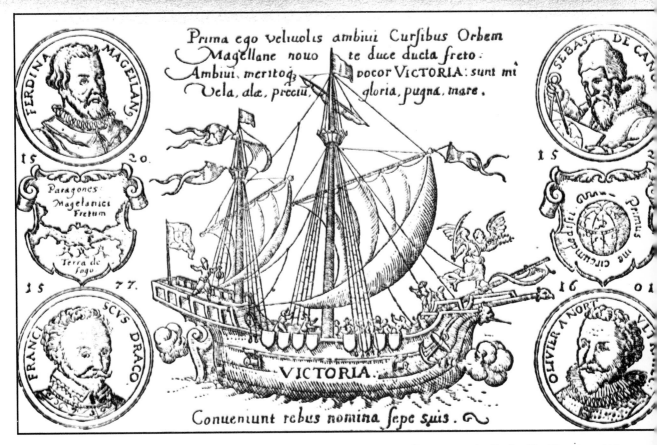

Prima ego veliuolis ambiui Curſibus Orbem
Magellane nouo te duce ducta freto:
Ambiui, meritoq̃ docor VICTORIA: sunt mi
Vela, alæ, preciũ, gloria, pugna, mare.

VICTORIA

Conueniunt rebus nomina ſæpe ſuis.

Carvalho's leadership, they became pirates, stealing treasures from lightly armed Oriental vessels.

By the fall of 1521, however, the crew had had enough of Carvalho. They elected Gonzalo Gómez de Espinosa as the new commander of the fleet. Espinosa was a just commander, but he had no talent to lead his crew back to Spain. Eventually, he, too, met his downfall. While the *Trinidad* was beached for repairs, he and his men were captured by Portuguese sailors and hanged as pirates.

Of the five ships in the original fleet, only the *Victoria* survived. It was commanded by Juan Sebastián del Cano, one of the San Julián mutiny leaders. Despite his shadowy past, he proved a worthy captain. He sailed the *Victoria* more than ten thousand miles, most of it through hostile Portuguese territory, back to Spain.

Magellan's ship Victoria, *which completed the circumnavigation of the globe without him.*

On September 6, 1522, eighteen survivors aboard the *Victoria* sailed into the Spanish harbor of Sanlúcar de Barrameda. Oddly enough, the men on board were convinced that it was really September 7. Some had kept a careful record of the passing days and years. Only decades later was it understood that traveling around the world meant losing or gaining a full day. By then an international dateline was established for such travelers.

For many years, Magellan was denied his true place in history. By an odd twist of fate, King Manuel died shortly after Magellan was killed. The vengeful king never learned the outcome of the great voyage nor of Magellan's death. When news of the voyage around the world became widely known in Portugal, Magellan was regarded by many as a traitor. They felt he should have sailed under the Portuguese flag.

Not even the Spaniards gave Magellan the credit he deserved. Of the men who survived the voyage, only

Title page for two accounts of Magellan's voyage, by Maximillian of Transylvania and Antonio Pigafetta, published in 1536

IL VIAGGIO
FATTO DA GLI SPA
GNIVOLI A
TORNO A'L
MONDO.

Con Gratia per Anni. XIIII.

M D X X X VI.

Drawing from a published version of Pigafetta's account, showing the catamaran (outrigger boat) used by some of the Pacific islanders

Antonio Pigafetta spoke well of him. The others, eager to hide their own treason, made up lies about Magellan. Even Pigafetta, in order not to offend King Charles, was forced to make a number of changes in his diary. He altered the facts to protect the Spanish captains.

For years afterward, Magellan was judged harshly by Europeans who heard stories of the great adventure. Antonio Pigafetta, on the other hand, became one of the most famous men in Europe because of his diary. Kings and queens, and even the pope, demanded to hear about the historic voyage. In 1524, he fled from these royal commands to become a monk in a quiet religious community—where he was promptly asked for a copy of the great diary!

The diary was first published in 1524, and many editions followed. It has lasted through the centuries, shedding fair light on perhaps the greatest explorer the world has ever known—Ferdinand Magellan.

Appendices: Maps

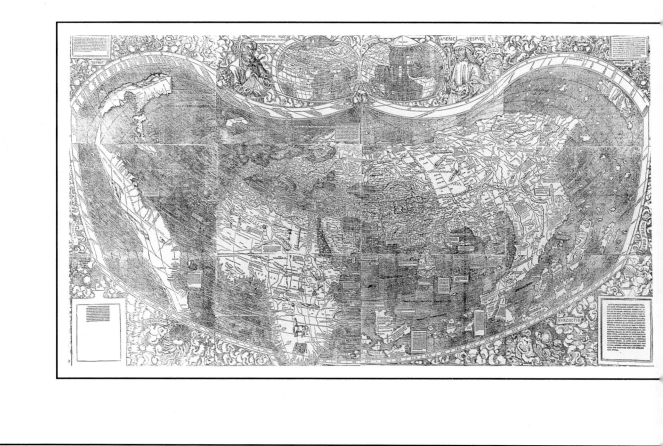

Above: World map of 1507, one of the first to use the name "America" to describe the New World. At this point, only the easternmost portion of the Americas— the strip of land at the left—had been discovered.

Opposite page: A map dating from around 1520, showing what was known of South America and the Caribbean at the time

116

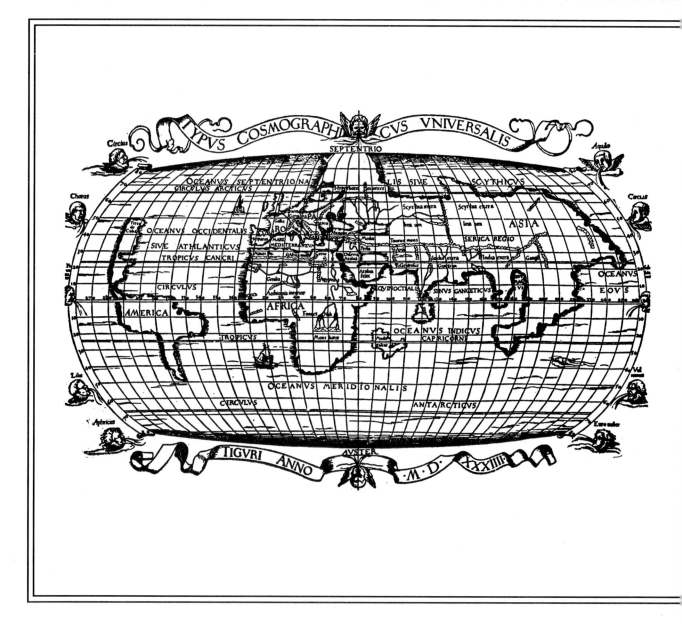

Above: Woodcut of a world map published in 1534

Opposite page: Ruysch's map of 1508, one of the earliest engraved maps of the New World. It shows such recently discovered lands as Cuba, the Bahamas, Hispaniola, parts of North America, and the north coast of South America.

A 1506 map of the world by Italian geographers
Matheo Contarini and Francesco Roselli. Europe, and
even Africa, appear in detail, while South America is
largely a blank mass of land at the upper left-hand part
of the map.

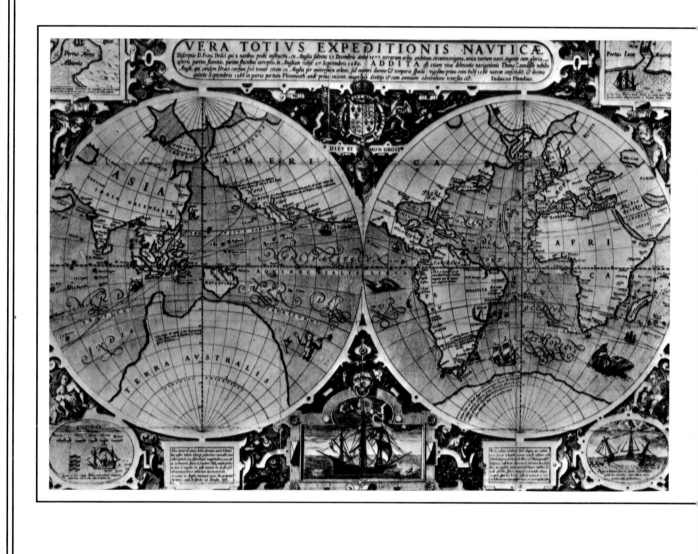

Map engraved by Jodacus Hondius around 1590. It shows the routes of the next two circumnavigations of the globe after Magellan's: those of Englishmen Francis Drake (1577–1580) and Thomas Cavendish (1586–1588).

Timeline of Events in Magellan's Lifetime

Around 1480—Ferdinand Magellan is born, probably near Braga, Portugal.

1480—End of Tatar rule in Russia ; Ivan III establishes new Russian empire.

1481—The Christian Church and the Spanish crown institute the Spanish Inquisition.

1487—Southern India's Muslim Bahmani dynasty begins to break up into five independent Muslim kingdoms.

1488—Bartholomeu Dias sails around the Cape of Good Hope, Africa's southern tip.

1491—Granada, the last Muslim outpost in Spain, is conquered.

1492—Christopher Columbus, sailing for Spain, reaches the Bahamas in the New World. Muslims and Jews are driven out of Spain.

1494—In the Treaty of Tordesillas, Spain and Portugal divide the New World between them.

1497—John Cabot discovers the North American continent, probably at Labrador.

1498—Vasco da Gama sails around Africa and reaches India, opening up direct European trade with the Orient. Columbus discovers the South American mainland on his third voyage.

1499—Guru Nanak, founder of the Sikh religion, begins preaching. Amerigo Vespucci sails across the Atlantic Ocean to the coast of Venezuela.

1500—Pedro Cabral reaches the coast of Brazil and claims it for Portugal. The Amazon River is discovered.

1502—Columbus explores the coast of Panama on his fourth voyage.

1503—Spain begins slave trade in the New World.

1504—French fishermen reach the coast of Newfoundland.

1507—Leo Africanus, an Arab, reaches West Africa.

1509—Henry VIII becomes King of England.

1511—Afonso de Albuquerque, Portuguese viceroy of India, captures Malacca on the Indian Ocean. Velázquez conquers Cuba and founds Havana.

1512—Michelangelo finishes painting his frescoes on the ceiling of Rome's Sistine Chapel. Nicholas Copernicus states that the earth and the other planets revolve around the sun.

1513—Italian Prince Machiavelli writes *Il Principe* (*The Prince*), an influential political work. Ponce de León discovers Florida. Vasco de Balboa discovers the Pacific Ocean.

1515—Afonso de Albuquerque captures the city of Ormuz on the Persian Gulf.

1516—Juan de Solis discovers the Río de la Plata.

1517—Protestant Reformation begins when German cleric Martin Luther issues his 95 Theses in Wittenberg, Germany.

1518—Kings of England and France hold "summit meeting."

1519—Ferdinand Magellan begins his voyage to circumnavigate the globe. Ulrich Zwingli begins the Reformation in Zurich, Switzerland.

1520—Magellan sails through the Strait of Magellan and enters the Pacific Ocean. Suleiman the Magnificent becomes sultan of the Ottoman (Turkish) Empire.

1521—Hernando Cortés conquers Mexico's Aztec Indians, beginning Spain's colonial empire in Mexico. Ferdinand Magellan is killed while trying to capture the Pacific island of Mactan.

Glossary of Terms

astrolabe—A navigational instrument used to determine latitude

caravel—A sailing ship with three masts and square or triangular sails

cargo—Goods carried on a ship

circumnavigate—To sail or travel all the way around something

constellation—A pattern that seems to be formed by a group of stars

continent—One of the seven great masses of land on the globe

court-martial—A trial by a military court

customhouse—A building where ships' goods are unloaded and taxed

dhow—An Arab boat with a long, overhanging forward section

doldrums—An area of the ocean near the equator where the winds are often calm

equator—An imaginary line around the earth, dividing it equally into north and south halves

expedition—A trip taken for a special purpose, such as finding something

fleet—A group of ships sailing together

head winds—Winds blowing in the opposite direction from a ship's course

junk—A Chinese ship with tall poles as masts

latitude—Imaginary east-to-west lines around the earth that indicate distance north or south of the equator

malnutrition—The condition of a person who is not receiving the proper foods

maritime—Having to do with the sea and sailing

massacre—To cruelly kill and destroy on a large scale

mirage—A visual effect often seen at sea, in deserts, or on hot pavements, caused by the bending of light rays

monastery—A residence for monks (men who belong to a religious order)

mutiny—A rebellion of a ship's crew against the captain

navigation—The science of ship or air travel ; it includes the study of how to find location, direction of travel, and distance traveled

outrigger—A log attached to the side of a canoe to prevent its turning over

peppercorns—The dried berries of the East Indian pepper plant ; peppercorns can be ground to produce pepper in flake or powder form

plague—A severe, widespread, contagious disease caused by a bacterium

putrid—Rotten

rajah—A prince or chief in India or Malaya

rations—Food carried aboard a ship for the sailors to eat

reef—A ridge of rocks or sand just below the surface of the water

sampan—A flat-bottomed Chinese sailboat

scurvy—A disease caused by a lack of vitamin C

strait—A narrow strip of water between two larger bodies of water

viceroy—The governor of a country or province who represents the king

Bibliography

For further reading, see :

Guillemard, Francis H. *The Life of Ferdinand Magellan and the First Circumnavigation of the Globe.* New York : AMS Press, 1971. Reprint of 1890 edition.

Nowell, Charles E., ed. *Magellan's Voyage Around the World : Three Contemporary Accounts.* Evanston, IL : Northwestern University Press, 1962.

Parr, Charles M. *So Noble A Captain : The Life and Times of Ferdinand Magellan.* Westport, CT : Greenwood Press, 1976. Reprint of 1953 edition.

Pigafetta, Antonio. *Magellan's Voyage : A Narrative Account of the First Circumnavigation.* 2 vols. New Haven, CT : Yale University Press, 1969.

Sanderlin, George. *First Around the World : A Journal of Magellan's Voyage.* New York : Harper & Row, 1964.

Syme, Ronald. *Magellan : First Around the World.* New York : William Morrow, 1953.

Wilkie, Katherine. *Ferdinand Magellan : Noble Captain.* Boston, MA : Houghton Mifflin, Piper Books, 1963.

Index

Page numbers in boldface type indicate illustrations.

Picture Identifications for Chapter Opening Spreads

6–7—Ptolemy's map of the world

14–15—The first large map of the New World (see land at left), made by Spanish navigator Juan de la Cosa around 1500

28–29—The port of Lisbon in the sixteenth century

40–41—Sixteenth-century Lisbon, as seen from the Tagus River

56–57—Engraving of a ship in stormy waters

68–69—The Strait of Magellan at sunset

88–89—Magellan's fleet

108–109—Map of the world from the *Theatrum Orbis Terrarum* of Flemish mapmaker Abraham Ortellius (1570), the first bound volume of maps intended as an atlas

Acknowledgment

For a critical reading of the manuscript, our thanks to John Parker, Ph.D., Curator, James Ford Bell Library, University of Minneapolis, Minneapolis, Minnesota

About the Author

Jim Hargrove has worked as a writer and editor for more than 10 years. After serving as an editorial director for three Chicago area publishers, he began a career as an independent writer, preparing a series of books for children. He has contributed to works by nearly 20 different publishers. Some of his Childrens Press titles are *Mark Twain : The Story of Samuel Clemens, Gateway to Freedom : The Story of the Statue of Liberty and Ellis Island, The Story of the Black Hawk War,* and *Microcomputers at Work.* With his wife and teenage daughter, he lives in a small Illinois town near the Wisconsin border.